THE GOSPEL OF FIRE

THE GOSPEL OF FIRE

STRATEGIES FOR FACING YOUR FEARS, CONFRONTING YOUR DEMONS, AND FINDING YOUR PURPOSE

ELIOT MARSHALL

LIONCREST

PUBLISHING

THE GOSPEL OF FIRE
*Strategies for Facing Your Fears, Confronting
Your Demons, and Finding Your Purpose*

ISBN   978-1-5445-0167-3 *Paperback*
        978-1-5445-0168-0 *Ebook*

To everyone who is struggling: please know that you are not alone. Know that someone else is out there struggling just like you. Know that you will get through this, and you have the ability to find greatness. I know this sounds impossible. Find one thing in your life to be grateful for and focus on that. I promise you will find another and another after that. After you have three things, go make someone else grateful for something. Then you will have four things for yourself. Do it again and again.

To those of you not struggling: realize how blessed and lucky you are. Realize that you now have one job and one job only. Go sprinkle some of that luck dust on someone who isn't so lucky. Find someone whose life you can make better. Don't tell them what to do—bring them along with you and show them exactly how to do it. You will become even more blessed and luckier.

To my parents: my goal every day is to try to be as good as a parent as you were to me and Ita. People ask for a lot of things in their lives, but nobody got more than me because I had two parents who loved me and did everything for me. I love you guys, and I will never be able to pay the tab.

To Ita: I'm sure growing up with me wasn't easy. I wouldn't have wanted to do it with someone else, though. As much as I drove you crazy, you put up with me, and I love you.

To Renee: I'm not sure what to say other than you are my ride or die. I will ride this ride until the wheels fall off.

To Ian, Mike, Will, and Todd: I will never be able to repay you for what you did for me.

To all of my students: I thank you for spending your time with me. Time is the only thing in life we can't get more of. Your choice to spend yours with me will never be lost on me.

To Gale: I know you were just doing your job. It didn't feel like that to me, however. I felt and still feel like you truly care. Maybe you are used to 250 pound guys crying on your couch, but I'm not very used to doing that. Thank you!

To Amal: You gave me the gift of Jiu-Jitsu. You taught me and allowed me to grow in a way that I achieved great success. More importantly, outside of my mom, dad, sister, and maybe four others, I have nothing in my life without Jiu-Jitsu. Therefore, I have nothing in my life without you.

CONTENTS

INTRODUCTION

*" Life is about fighting. You're going to
have to fight every day of your life. "*
—RENZO GRACIE

What the fuck am I doing? I thought. *This is brutal. Why am
I doing this to myself?* I paced the floor frantically, looking
out of my hotel window and down onto the Las Vegas
Strip. The glow. All the people partying. All their noisy
exuberance, their fun—none of which I was experiencing
as I sat in my room, overcome with terror, and physically
and mentally exhausted from an eight-week training
camp. And now, from fight week, where I'd intentionally
been dehydrating myself to make weight.

I couldn't get my last fight out of my mind. I'd mentally
given up and I got my ass kicked. I took the beating, like
you're supposed to when you fight in the UFC, and I went

to the hospital after the match. For that fight, I hadn't had an eight-week camp to prepare; I had only ten days. It wasn't enough, and I was mentally checked out before I even stepped into the cage. It hurt—in a lot of ways.

There, in that hotel room over the bright Vegas lights, I was terrified it would happen again. I knew I was fighting a competitor who was even better than my last opponent. I didn't know how I'd react in that critical moment: *Would I check out? Would he get the better of me?* I moved throughout the room frantically, crying and scared shitless. My wife, Renee, tried to comfort me, but she couldn't console me. I knew I was worrying her; she'd never seen me this way, and we'd been through lots of fights.

"Look," she said. "Why don't you just go out there, get hit one time, and fall down. Be done. You're already here. You get thirty grand to walk in the cage and take a jab. You've done the work. Then let's go home."

Fuck it, I thought. *That's my plan.*

I knew it meant I'd be a mockery. I knew I might not even be able to do Jiu-Jitsu anymore, and Jiu-Jitsu was—and is—my life. I knew I'd embarrass myself. I knew I'd disappoint everyone who had come out of the woodwork, everyone who looked up to me as the guy who made it big as the best fighter to come out of our martial arts school, everyone who put me on this pedestal I wasn't even sure I wanted to be on.

Fighting was and is pressure, and it felt heavier than it ever had before. When the moment came to step into the cage, I had no expectation of winning. I did as planned: I took the jab to the face, but I only tripped backward. I didn't fall. Then I felt a switch go off in my brain.

There goes that idea, I thought. *Let's fucking fight.*

And fight I did. In fact, I had the fight of my life. After two rounds, it was pretty even and I went to my corner.

"Well, Fire Marshall," said my coach, Greg Jackson, calling me by my nickname, "you tell me what you've got left. Come on. You got anything for me? This could be it. It all comes down to this."

I felt an overwhelming calm come over me—a strange sensation in such an intense moment. A moment when I was literally fighting for not only my livelihood but also my life.

I got off the stool and I beat the brakes off the guy. I didn't even know who I was. I dropped him with punches and broke his arm; he couldn't fight for eleven months. Somehow, in the decision, the judges said I lost, but I didn't give a shit. To me, I'd won. With everything screaming at me to be a coward, to give in, to surrender—I didn't. Before that moment, I'd felt like I was in a prison. Afterward, I was free.

HELL: THE PRISON OF YOUR EGO

You may feel like you're in your own prison, whether you're held down by your job, your family, your health—anything. I'm not religious; I do, however, believe there's something greater than us and I believe in hell. Not the hell that comes after we die, though—the hell that's coming for us now. Today? Maybe—but one thing is certain: at some point in your life, hell is going to come for you, and it's going to be brought on by yourself. By your ego. By your thoughts. Whatever brings it on, just know that when it comes, you're going to have to fight. Grit your teeth, look it straight in the eye, and say, "Not today." My coach asked me what I had left as I sat on that stool, and life is going to ask the same of you many times. I know it has of me.

I never had a "ride off into the sunset" moment in my life or in my fighting career. In the past, worry and anxiety have sapped the energy from everything as I fixated on the image of how tough I was supposed to be. The harder I held on to that ideal, the more it crumbled, and the harder hell came for me. I learned to look the devil straight in his eyes. I learned how to face him, and when you do that, he turns the other way and runs. I know because I've been there.

I encourage you to go as deep into hell as you can. That's the Gospel of Fire: walk into the base of the blaze, far below the licking red and orange flames, and into the deep blue. Find the source and face it. Life is tough, man. Just when you think you can't go anymore, go anyway. I'm going to help you by telling you what my hell was like. I'm going to show you how I'm *still* scared of going back because I'm a human being, but I'm down to go again. I'll go there with you. That's what we need in our lives: true connections with other people.

My UFC fight that night didn't ultimately matter. Who cares about a Saturday-night fight that's barely legal? What does matter in the end is how we mitigate suffering for ourselves and how we help others mitigate suffering for themselves, too. What matters is how we do that *together*. That's why I wrote this book.

We are all swords in the process of being forged: we put the metal of our raw selves into the heat again and again. We bang on it. We abuse it. We melt it. We mold it. In the end, that sword is hard to break. Is the process easy? Hell no. Is it avoidable? Also no. Don't cower from your personal hell, but rise in spite of it. Be molded by it. This book will guide you in fearless living, something I've learned the hard way—which is the only way to learn it.

WHO AM I?

I'm what my friend Ryan Harris calls Obama black, which means my father is black and my mother is white. She's also Jewish, and her parents were concentration camp survivors. The stories my grandparents told me were so poignant that the air in their house felt still—tinged with the remnants of massive suffering. Still, though, they gave me so much love; my whole family did. In my childhood, I grew up surrounded by love and attention, and I never wanted for anything—at home, that is.

Socially, it was a different story. I spent my teen and young-adult years in a small South Jersey town where it wasn't exactly kosher to be mixed race. I didn't fit in. I didn't have friends. It was shitty. Really shitty.

As soon as I could, I moved away. I liked skiing, so I thought I'd attend the University of Colorado in Boulder. I also continued to pursue my love of martial arts and became the first American to win gold at the Pan American games for Brazilian Jiu-Jitsu in blue, purple (twice), and brown belt categories. This accomplishment was huge; I moved on to MMA, was cast in a reality TV show, and fought in the UFC for four years. Today, I'm a successful entrepreneur and own six martial arts schools in the Denver area. I'm also competing again and donating the money to charities and organizations that help those who suffer from anxiety and depression—the combination of which, especially the former, almost broke me. I'll share the story of my breakdown in chapter 1, and how even with all my success—a loving family, retirement from the UFC, a successful career as an entrepreneur—anxiety nearly caused my life to fall apart. The devil got ahold of me, and I had to fight my way out. But I didn't do it easily and I didn't do it alone. There is no such thing as "picking yourself up by your bootstraps." I was surrounded by support, and I want to give some of that back in the following pages.

In this book, I'll show you how to be a beast. How not to be afraid of your weaknesses—or, if you are, how not to give a fuck and go deal with them anyway. I'll show you how to be vulnerable, commit, and live in the moment. You'll see why every problem is actually a blessing, and you'll discover that it's ok to ask for help.

What I will not do in this book is judge or shame you. I will also not complain about my past. Yes, as I said earlier, I'm a black Jew who experienced racism—good. It made me stronger. I will not tell you how special I am or how special you are. Why? It's simple: nobody is special. We are all unique, but *special* has a connotation of entitlement. You aren't owed anything, but you still should be happy. And you can be, even if it doesn't feel like it right now. Getting there will not be easy, but in the end, you'll love the hardness. You'll love the struggle. In the range of our human experience, there will be all kinds of weather: rainy times, days when it's beautifully sunny, stormy seasons, and everything in between. *That's* what is special—the fact that no matter what the universe throws our way, we do hard shit. We face the fire, we conquer it, and we do it all together.

As the granddaddy of UFC fight week, Burt Watson used to scream as we walked the tunnel to the cage, "This is your fight, your night. Now, let's get it right! It's time to roll to the hole, baby!"

Let's go.

Chapter

ONE

FROM BREAKDOWN TO BREAKTHROUGH

> *"The world breaks everyone, and afterwards,*
> *some are strong at the broken places."*
>
> —ERNEST HEMINGWAY

There was a time that, while physically strong on the outside, I felt mentally defeated on the inside. Looking at me, though, it would have been hard to tell. My life was great: my businesses were successful, I drove a nice car, and I lived in a big house. I had a wonderful wife and two amazing kids.

The dream, right? Yes—and yet, I struggled. All I could think about for a long time was, *Man, what if this all fuckin' falls apart?*

As it turned out, my material life didn't fall apart. Instead, I did—right after a vacation in Maui.

SLEEPLESSNESS AND STRUGGLE

I remember it vividly: it was two years ago, and my family had just returned from a vacation in Hawaii. We'd had a nice time. After we arrived home, though, I knew something was wrong: I couldn't sleep. At first, that seemed normal: there's a four-hour time difference between where we were and our home in Colorado, so it made sense that I'd have jet lag. I was going to bed at 11:00 p.m. in Maui, but that was 3:00 a.m. in Colorado. Given my anxiety at the time, I couldn't handle the transition.

I spent four or five nights pacing the house and panicking, panicking, panicking. That first week back, I slept only six hours. Prolonged sleep deprivation affects you physically and emotionally, but the mental anxiety was horrendous too. It got so bad that I would start worrying about sleeping that night at around eleven every *morning*. Then, as the evening approached in Colorado, I'd be filled with even more terror over facing another sleepless night.

One day not long after we'd returned, at the height of my sleeplessness, I had a breakdown. Renee was at work, and I was driving with my kids in the car. I took a big, long breath, and my oldest son asked, "Daddy, are you OK?"

At that moment, I realized I wasn't OK. I went home, gave my kids a game to keep them occupied, and called my mom.

She and my dad were in a restaurant when I called. They went outside, and both got on the phone with me, and I walked outside my house. Three people, two different locations—all standing outside on the phone. I broke down, bawling. I told them about the lack of sleep, the mental pain, and the anxiety. They responded calmly and told me to breathe. Despite their reassurance, I could hear the worry in their voices; they didn't know I'd been struggling so much. Nobody did! I'd had a little bit of anxiety when I was younger, but since then, I'd gone on to do "great things" and tackle scary challenges. I'd fought in a fucking cage! I finally told someone I didn't feel as strong as I looked.

Pretty soon, the intensity passed, and I had to pull myself together to go back inside. I had a two-and-a-half-year-old and a six-year-old in the house; I couldn't just leave them alone for an extended period while I freaked out. I knew I needed to hold it together for my kids, and I knew my wife would be home soon. I looked out the window over and over, willing her car to pull up.

Finally, Renee arrived, and I called my doctor. I'm extremely fortunate that my doctor is one of my best friends. Even though it was a Friday night around 5:00 pm, I was able to get help immediately. He called in prescriptions for Xanax (an antianxiety medication), sleeping pills, and Lexapro (an antidepressant). I also started going to therapy twice a week.

Once I got on the meds and into therapy, things didn't turn around right away. During my months-long breakdown, I had to call my friends and take both Xanax and sleeping pills every single night to get to sleep. For comparison, consider this: if you take half a milligram of Xanax when you're doing well, it will knock you out. But I was working through so much anxiety in that period of my life, I could take twice that much, plus two prescription sleeping pills, and still be wide awake. That's how deep my hell was.

Jet lag shouldn't have been such a huge deal, but that's what anxiety does to you: it creates nonsensical, irrational responses. You can't just snap out of it. Some circuit trips, and you can't think straight. I couldn't stop thinking about whether or not I'd sleep—and most of the time, I didn't. At around 11:00 p.m., I would have a panic attack, run to the basement, and call one of my three friends or sometimes my sister. If it was a particularly rough night, I'd talk to them until they had to get some sleep, then I'd struggle a couple more hours until I could call my mom, who was on the East Coast and an early riser.

Everything was a struggle. I tried to be present for Renee and the kids, but it was extremely hard. My boys were little, so they were shielded from what was going on for the most part. My wife, on the other hand, saw everything that was happening. She tried to be there for me and support me, but I wouldn't have blamed her for wondering where our relationship was going sometimes. She doesn't have anxiety like I do, so it's hard for her to fully understand. She tried to keep life moving along as normally as possible, but that normalcy still triggered me. If she made weekend plans, for example, it completely blindsided me.

I'd think, *What the fuck do you mean we're going out with friends on Friday night? I don't even know if I'm going to be here on Friday night!* Don't get me wrong: it's not that I was by any means suicidal—I couldn't even think that far ahead. I was trying to survive each moment, and that was all I could do. I couldn't think about Friday when it was Wednesday. At the time, that seemed absurd to me.

JOURNALING MY WAY OUT

As I grappled with all the fear, anxiety, and insomnia, I started journaling. I'd write out my worst-case scenario if I couldn't sleep. I would play out the story of what not sleeping would look like. Oftentimes, it looked like this:

I'm not going to sleep tonight, and then I'm not going to sleep tomorrow. And then when I don't sleep for enough days in a row, I'm going to go crazy. When I go crazy, I'm not going to be able to take care of my kids. Renee will put up with it for a little bit. Eventually, she's not going to be able to put up with the situation, because who the fuck wants to live like that?

When she gets tired of putting up with me, she's going to leave me. We'll get a divorce. We'll have to go to court, and then she's going to bring all of my mental health struggles up, including how I can't take care of the kids. Then I'm not going to be able to see my kids. If I can't be with my kids, I'm going to fucking kill myself.

The end.

None of what I was writing was actually true or came to pass, but it helped to write out the worst possible catastrophe I could imagine. I had so much toxic shit in my head, and I needed to *get it out* instead of letting it spin around and around in there. For me, putting it on paper made it less scary. Was it a fun activity? Hell no. It was painful, but I had to do it to take away some of the power from my fears.

Eventually—through a combination of medication, therapy, journaling, and the support of family and friends—I was able to recover. It took saying I wasn't OK to finally get to a place where I could actually *be* OK. Still, it was a long road.

ON THE UPSIDE

I know that I'm extremely blessed to have had the kind of help I had at my fingertips on a moment's notice. Not everyone can call their doctor on a Friday night and get the medication or support they need. If this is you, your only option might be going to the emergency room. Even that won't necessarily work, because the doctors might think you're simply seeking drugs. I was lucky to be able to get immediate help.

I was also fortunate that my therapist could get me in quickly and that I could afford to go to appointments every week, sometimes twice a week. At first, I'd spend the whole time crying, but I improved slowly. I still sing the praises of therapy, and I still go. Taking the time to focus on mental health is completely worth it.

That lesson is clear to me now, but learning it was painful. It took nine months to get through that massive breakdown. After overcoming that low point, I began to think about how I'd gotten there in the first place.

ROOT CAUSES: MY FIRST SENSE OF DREAD

When I was eight years old, my family was building a new house in a new town. I had great parents who protected me from the hard things in life at that age, as parents should. I'd heard about the Holocaust and knew that my grandparents had been in the concentration camps, but I'd heard only little fragments of stories. I hadn't heard all the details, and I was too young to really comprehend their experiences.

One day, we drove up to our house, and it had been spray-painted. My first thought was that the painters had done terrible work; I didn't truly comprehend what was going on—that is, until we got closer. Then I could see crudely painted words surrounded by swastikas: "Nigers go home." They'd misspelled the slur, but we got the picture. Even at that age, I had a feeling of what it all meant. The main question in my mind was, *Why?* We hadn't done anything to anybody. We just liked the neighborhood and wanted to move in.

My mom was angry; she hadn't experienced much blatant prejudice. She's Jewish, but that's a pretty hard heritage to identify just by looking at someone. People weren't walking up to her on a regular basis and saying, "kike." My dad, on the other hand, is black. You can see his background on his face. How can he hide it? He was born in 1948, grew up very poor, and came of age during the civil rights movement. He remembers segregation, when water fountains were labeled by race. He'd experienced this kind of blatant prejudice his whole life. Even as a kid, I could see the difference between their reactions. My dad seemed accustomed to this type of treatment, but my mom didn't handle it well.

Our old neighborhood had been poor, rural, and white, but we didn't experience such blatant racism. When we moved to the new neighborhood, only twenty or thirty minutes away, it seemed like a better place. I was just a kid, and up until the vandalism, everything had seemed like it was hunky-dory. I didn't understand all the bad things hiding in the world—that was the first moment I realized things were more complicated than they seemed.

PREPARING FOR THE WORST

I grew up around people who always prepared for the worst. My dad grew up during a time of civil unrest, and my mom's parents survived the Holocaust. Their experiences growing up were much different. My mom's parents—my *baba* and *zeide* in Yiddish—were able to protect her more than my dad was protected. When I went to school, my mom told me to behave and concentrate. My dad told me to watch my back. Those were the messages I received every single day.

My baba and zeide clung to the idea that even so-called

friends who ate at your table might turn you in to the Nazis one day. They knew from experience that they couldn't trust anyone—other Jews in the concentration camp had fought them for a piece of bread. My zeide was the only one in his family to survive, and I could still feel the pain and the distrust in him. According to him, your neighbor will betray you. You were on your own with only your immediate family to rely on. Almost no one came to their house.

The adults around me had come from a lot of hardship, so they had a different frame of reference. My dad talked about not having running water as a child and needing to heat up water for a bath. A big theme in my family was "No one died today." Your day couldn't have been that bad if no one had died. If you'd eaten, slept, and been sheltered from the cold, what could you complain about? Their main goal was to keep me safe, and they always emphasized it. One result was that I started to wonder what I was being kept safe *from*. What was going to threaten my safety? That question resulted in some deep-seated anxiety.

NEVER BELONGING

We lived in Franklinville, New Jersey, which was rural and spread out. My house sat on four acres or so. All the kids in school knew one another, moved up in grades together, and had their seemingly preassigned roles in sports. If they played a position in middle school, they were going to play that position in high school. New kids almost never joined. We were outsiders.

I didn't have friends in school and wasn't popular. When kids in my class circulated lists ranking the cutest and best people, I was always at the bottom of every list—one of which was hung on the blackboard by a teacher. I felt like I couldn't win. That kind of treatment was an everyday experience for me and continued into high school, and I ate lunch by myself every day. It was a heavy kind of loneliness; all I wanted was to have friends. Looking back, maybe that desperation was part of the problem.

I didn't have any day-to-day experience of connecting with my peers as I was growing up, and it was tough. I did have three friends total, but none went to my school. One was a neighbor, the other was a friend from karate who lived in a different town, and the other also went to karate and was four years older than me. Martial arts was my only outlet.

The state of my early life brought on a lot of anxiety. I stayed up late at night worrying and hated going to school. There were also things I did that did not help. I was ashamed of being chunky with baby fat, so I tried not to let my clothing size go up. In my head, bigger clothes meant I was getting fatter. Sizing down did not have the intended effect, exactly the opposite: wearing overly tight clothing is not a good look. It only invites more bullying. To this day, I have an obsession with not being fat. It has not gone away. If my weight goes up a little bit, it brings up bad feelings.

My sister had struggles similar to mine, only more so. At a certain point, your parents can do only so much for you, and your network of support has to switch to your peers. I was lucky to at least have martial arts, but my sister didn't have anything. The experience was extremely difficult for her. She went into a downward spiral for five to ten years. That, in turn, put a lot of stress on our family. I trace it all back to how little we were accepted in our town.

We didn't face horrible racism as kids—white kids weren't running around calling us niggers and kikes—but even worse than that, my sister and I weren't accepted by *anybody*. There were some black kids in my school, but they weren't my friends. There were some Jewish kids, but they weren't my friends either. My family was educated, and I was in honors classes. I was the only black kid in those classes, which only emphasized the racial and socioeconomic divide I felt.

In the end, we were nothing. My sister and I had only

each other. When I graduated, I knew one thing for sure: I wanted out.

A FRESH START: CU, BOULDER

After graduation, I headed to college at the University of Colorado, Boulder, and had a great freshman year. I made friends and was rather popular. At eighteen, I got my first real girlfriend. I also got laid for the first time. I was a late bloomer; most people have all these great experiences much earlier than I did.

I felt amazing that first year of college. On my flight out to Colorado, I remember promising myself that I was going to change my life, and I did. Nobody knew who I was, and I felt I could start over. I'd lost the baby fat and was in shape. No one had to know that up to that point, I wasn't liked and didn't have friends. I had a clean slate, and I used it. Life got easier for me—I felt like I'd wanted to feel in high school.

For some people, high school goes great. Then, once they turn eighteen, life is never that great again. I went to school with a lot of kids in that situation. They never left the town, and many of them didn't do much after graduating. Being quarterback or homecoming queen was the high point of their life. I didn't have that problem, though. My freshman year of college was badass. Ten of my friends all lived together in the same dorm. My girlfriend lived right down the hall. We ate dinner together every night. It was like a big, happy family, except without parents around to tell us what to do. It was a fun experience, and I was riding high—until things changed.

IT ALL FALLS APART

When sophomore year rolled around, my situation felt different. We weren't living in the dorm anymore; we all had our own places. We didn't spend time together like we had in the past. At first, I was still with my girlfriend, but then we broke up. She worked at Chili's and was able to sneak everyone alcohol. There were times when my friends would drop me off at home and go drink with her. I'd be alone; it felt like high school again.

I was feeling rejected once again, just like I had in high school. But something else was about to happen that would deeply affect me more: my baba got sick and died very quickly. It's hard to explain how close my baba and I were. Growing up, I saw her three or four times a week, every week. She did everything for me. Later, when I was in college, she was approaching seventy years old. Still, she'd slave over a hot stove to prepare the foods I loved for me when I came home. That's what Holocaust-surviving families do—they trust family and only family. My zeide would often say to me, "Eliot, when it comes down to it, they're either going to hide you from the Nazis or turn you in to the Nazis. The Nazis are going to come again, so who can you trust?"

When my baba died, it was a huge blow. My zeide knew how to deal with it, because he'd already seen so many people die. But it was extremely hard on my mom, my uncle, my sister, and me. I had two panic attacks on the day of her funeral and couldn't go to the service. Instead, I had to go to the hospital.

My life was crumbling around me: my baba had died, and my social support system was falling apart. My friends were dropping me off to go drink with my fucking ex-girlfriend. One night, I came home to find that my roommates had moved out of our shared apartment. They'd bounced without saying anything to me. They left the state and stuck me with the lease. To make extra money to cover the rent, I had to start working more and sleeping less. With multiple jobs, school, and the loss of my baba, I wasn't able to sleep well at all. With all the stress, my panic attacks returned.

I needed an outlet, and I found one in Jiu-Jitsu. I'll share the entire story in chapter 6, but let's just say this was one of the many times the sport would save my life.

LOSING MY TOUGH IMAGE

Because my sister and I had a difficult time growing up in New Jersey, we struggled to find real friends. I turned to martial arts as a solution; I decided people were going to like me because of how tough I was. I leaned into that image really fucking hard.

Fighting and gaining social status for my toughness got me into wanting to fight in the UFC—and I did. But the cage doesn't lie; I got beat up sometimes. I wasn't the champion. I obviously wasn't the toughest. In the end, I was released from the UFC. I got cut; I didn't choose to retire.

Getting fired sparked another internal struggle—my image of who I was fell apart. I started to worry my whole life could collapse; I could lose my relationships, my business, everything. Ultimately, I believe the anxiety from losing my tough image of myself—and all the events that led up to my having it in the first place—triggered the breakdown.

GETTING THROUGH THE BREAKDOWN

I can point to possible causes of my anxiety, but in the end, the causes don't really matter. The causes are in the past. When you have anxiety, your most important task is figuring out how you're going to get through it. Now.

When I started having a breakdown in my thirties, my first step toward recovery was admitting that I needed real help. I couldn't beat down what was happening by myself like I had before. Even if I could have, I'd lived long enough to realize my anxiety was going to keep popping back up and rearing its ugly head, no matter what I did. Reaching out to my mom and my doctor was a huge first step. I'd never wanted to take medication before, but my situation had gotten so bad that the doctor didn't even have to try to persuade me. He simply reminded me that I'd been fighting the same battle for a long time. He was both a doctor and a friend. He knew I was too tired to continue to fight; my attitude at that point was simple I was going to do whatever it took to make the anxiety stop.

For me, that meant medication, therapy, journaling, and telling my story—one of the most powerful antidotes to anxiety I've found. When I started writing down my fears and talking to people about them, I saw I wasn't alone. And neither are you. I'll share my discoveries throughout this book, but first, here are a few lessons I've learned that you might find useful right away:

JUST GET THROUGH TODAY

Early on in my bout with intense insomnia, Renee asked me a question that was key to my recovery.

"Why don't you just go about your day as if you'd slept? What's the plan for today?" she asked one morning. "Follow the plan."

Make long-term plans? No fucking way. Follow the plan for that *one day*? I felt like I could do that—so I did, over and over. This attitude got me out of the house and to the gym to teach Jiu-Jitsu. Otherwise, I would have been cooped up, obsessing about how tired I was and feeling like I should take a nap. Yes, it was true that I was tired, but telling myself that over and over again wasn't going to help. Staying in the house and avoiding everything would only build up phobias.

Still, I was *so* tired. I wasn't tired like I'd stayed up partying for a couple of days; I was completely exhausted. When you stay up partying, you're having fun. When you're up all night with anxiety, you are fighting back the devil. It takes everything you have. It's the most brutal fight I've ever had, and it was with myself.

On that same day, after I'd dragged myself to work, another member of my circle said something to me that stuck. Ian, one of my general managers, who's also one of my best friends, got me a cup of coffee.

"I can't drink that, man," I told him. "I won't sleep tonight."

"You're already not sleeping," he said. "Drink this so you can at least feel better for the next couple of hours. It's four o'clock right now. I'll be on the phone with you later tonight, so don't fucking worry about eleven o'clock right now. Just do four o'clock."

Then he sat there with me and watched me drink the coffee so I wouldn't dump it out.

The bottom line? When you're in the midst of a breakdown, you need someone who will ride or die with you. That's what Ian was doing—he was riding or dying with me. He helped me get through that moment and also assured me he'd be there for me later, too. He encouraged me to just get through the day. The moment. The *next thing*—whatever that looked like—instead of letting my fear of the future kill me.

STOP TRYING—GIVE UP CONTROL

When eleven o'clock came that night, Ian was on the phone with me, just like he said he'd be.

"Here's what you're going to do," he told me. "Go take your sleeping pills and go downstairs. Turn on the television and stay awake all night. Don't try to sleep. You've been trying to sleep so fucking hard. Stay awake and call me back in half an hour."

Half an hour came six hours later for me because I fell asleep. Why? I'd stopped trying. I gave up. To this day, I use the same strategy. I don't take sleeping pills anymore, but I get in bed and turn on *Law & Order*. I say to myself, *All right, I'm going to stay awake all night*. Usually, though, I close my eyes during the first commercial, and by the second one, I fall asleep. By not trying anymore, I took the power away from my problem.

When you let anxiety and depression take away your day, you feed into them. To recover, you have to take away their food. Renee didn't really know what she was doing when she told me to stick to my plan for the day as if I'd slept, but it was a good strategy. If I'd sat in the house doing nothing and dwelling on all my negative thoughts, I would have been feeding into the problem. Ian did the same thing by getting me to focus on staying awake instead of obsessing over how I needed to sleep. Together, they showed me how to stop feeding the demons.

CHANGE YOUR BEHAVIOR

Once anxiety or depression captures your thoughts, you have to figure out how to take them back. The key is changing your behavior. This approach is the basis of cognitive behavioral therapy. You actively address the question, "What will I do when these problems come up for me?"

I have strategies in place for when I can't sleep. I get out of bed and watch TV or listen to an audiobook. I decide to stay awake. I also follow the same rule I have for my kids: if I'm scared of something, I do it anyway. I flip the fear around in my head. *OK, let's see how bad things can be. Bring it on,* I think. Then I go about my day.

If you think I don't still have anxiety, you're wrong. I still deal with it. But when I feel it creeping up on me and just want to give up and chill in my house, I make myself go extra hard that day. I put all my chips on the table. I double down. I'm too busy "doing" to fall victim to it. I'm out living my life, doing what makes me human.

FIND YOUR GREATNESS

Whatever your past has, whether it's full of greatness or failure, it has nothing to do with your present—unless you let it. That choice is on you. How you deal with what other people do to you or the circumstances the universe sends your way is up to you. When you give that choice away and tell yourself you can't control your reactions, you give up your power.

I was a math major in college. Life can be broken down into a simple formula that my friend Brian Cain told me once: E + R = O. Events + Responses = Outcomes. There is only one variable you have any control over, and that is R.

Yes, life is tougher for some individuals than others. Socioeconomic factors and the unique circumstances of our upbringings can make things easier or harder for us. We should do everything we can to help each other, but when it comes down to the choice of how to react to your own situation, it's up to you.

You can do it. You have the power. You are great. Muhammad Ali said, "I'm going to show you how great I am." You can be great, too, and show everyone how great you are. You've got to find *your kind* of great, though. It's not going to be the same as Muhammad Ali's or Rosa Parks's kind of great. It's going to be different from Lebron James, Bill Gates, or Oprah Winfrey. It's going to be your own.

You may not recognize what makes you great. Maybe nobody else does either—yet. Twenty years ago, if someone told you Steve Jobs was going to be great, you would have thought they were nuts. A phone that's a computer I carry around in my hand? Give me a break. When Michael Jordan got cut from his high school basketball team, the starters made fun of him. All he wanted to do in his life was play, but if you'd told them he was going to be the greatest basketball player ever, they would have laughed at you.

So what? Great people don't let their past experiences define them. The greatest MMA fighter ever, in my opinion, is Anderson Silva. He was going to retire before he went into the UFC. He was not a top-tier fighter. He was fighting in the minor leagues, and in his last five fights, he was three and two—not stellar. His training partner and Jiu-Jitsu teacher, who was fighting in the UFC at the time, said, "I know you're struggling, but just do one fight in the UFC. Dana White will give you one fight."

Silva signed the contract for one fight, and he destroyed his opponent—to the point that they gave him an immediate title shot the next fight. He went on to win a crazy number of fights in a row: sixteen. Back when he originally planned to retire, people would have laughed at you if you'd said he was going to be one of the greatest fighters of all time. They would have been wrong.

Michael Jordan, Anderson Silva, Muhammad Ali, Steve Jobs, Oprah Winfrey—name any successful person. They each had unique challenges but found their greatness in spite of them, and you can too.

SILVER LININGS

My breakdown was fucking brutal, man. But it was a pivotal moment in my life, and I grew from the experience. These are some things I got from my dance with the devil.

WE'RE NOT SPECIAL

One of the silver linings of my breakdown was learning I'm not special. I'm not even special in the way I suffered; thousands of people suffer just like I did.

In the end, I'm grateful for my breakdown because it showed me who I was. I'd been wandering a bit as an individual. The experience helped me clarify everything I wanted to be in life. First and foremost, it helped me become a better dad. It also helped me become a better teacher. Now I know exactly who I am.

WE CAN BE BETTER PEOPLE

The day before my breakdown, the people in my life would have said I was a good father and a good teacher. I'm better now, though. The experience put me in touch with myself. When you understand yourself, you can spread your message in more meaningful ways. You can be more empathetic and sympathetic. You can be a better listener. You can be more vulnerable and see situations from the points of view of others.

FAILURE DOESN'T DEFINE US

My breakdown made me take a hard look at myself and my failures. What did I learn? Even my failures made me better. They don't define me, and they aren't actually losses. I no longer have that deep-seated fear of failure that is concerned with how others will see me. Nope. Instead, I think, *Sweet, now I get to try again, but differently.*

The truth is simple: I'm still human. Sometimes I blow it with my kids and get angry when I shouldn't. What parent doesn't? Who doesn't get frustrated? Sometimes I fail my students and say the wrong thing. Sometimes I let Renee down and say something mean that I know I shouldn't say.

In these situations and more, I understand I don't have to be right all the time. I'm much better and faster at saying, "I'm sorry." I can take the blame when things go wrong, and I can see that most of the time when things go right, it's not solely to my credit.

EVERY COIN HAS TWO SIDES

My breakdown taught me another critical lesson: to love my anxiety. I don't love it in the moment—*never* in the moment—but it's part of me. I don't hate the worst parts about myself anymore. I love them.

Ultimately, the things that make us terrible are also the things that make us great. They're the same traits. Obsessing and turning things over and over in my head allowed me to be great at Jiu-Jitsu, but those qualities are also what got me crying on my therapist's couch and pacing around my house in the middle of the night. For me, the qualities that lead to success and to anxiety are two sides of the same coin.

I am intense, driven to succeed, and I know that I owe my best to my family and my students. All positive, right? Yes, but they're also the things that keep me up at night. That's my point: you may think your great traits and your bad ones are different, but they're not. Don't wish any part of you away. Instead, learn to leverage those traits instead of letting them consume you in a negative way.

WE MUST MAKE SPACE FOR OTHERS

I'll always be working on my ego. The smaller it gets, the more room and time I have to consider how other people are doing, because I'm not so worried about myself. I know I'll be able to deal with whatever comes up for me, because I've survived hell, so I know I can survive it again. Now I can open up some space for others. The changes in my brain, life, and heart have allowed me to care more about other people. I wholeheartedly believe the only way to get through life is together. If you have time for only yourself, you're going to be let down.

You might not realize what you've been missing until the end of your life. A lot of champions have no friends because they're so wrapped up in their egos. When they look back on their lives when they're dying, they'll realize they're alone. Even incredibly successful people such as Steve Jobs come to the end of their lives with a lot of regret. He regretted he hadn't made more time for the people in his life. He didn't talk about the iPhone 7 in his last public comments. He talked about people.

Your accomplishments are not the most important parts of your life. Besides, any record you break will sooner or later be broken by someone else. Whether you excel in sports or in work, there will *always* be someone who comes along after you and does what you did but even better. The bar for success will only keep rising. It's satisfying to strive for something greater, but keep in mind that none of us will have really succeeded unless we've done something to touch another human being's soul. That's part of anxiety's gift to me: I can strive but also know when to calm down, realize how special *I'm not* and how great *I'm not*, and make room for people I didn't make time to understand before.

HOW TO HELP YOURSELF RIGHT NOW

Are you having a hard time? Maybe you're pacing every night or dealing with a brutal moment right now. Whatever your struggle looks like, ask yourself a simple question to help you over the hump: Can you do *this exact second*? Forget about the next five minutes; I'm talking about the next second, literally. Can you do it? Remember when Ian gave me the coffee? He didn't want me to worry about later that night; he knew I needed to focus on four o'clock.

When we get wrapped up in our own anxiety, it can be hard to see anything but what we think is wrong. When you just do *right now* and don't worry about anything else, some of the pressure gets released. Ask yourself what you would like to do this second, and then do it. Don't aim high—choose something doable in this moment. Don't try to be better in this second. Better is going to take a while. Still, you can do *something*. Go for a walk. Clean your room. Brush your teeth. Take a shower. Fill your time.

As you're doing *right now*, remember you don't have to do it by yourself. You're not alone, even if it feels that way. Pick up the phone and call somebody. Be honest. Tell somebody you're in hell. They'll help you.

When I meditate with my sons, we have a saying at the end. "Let your thoughts come and go. Let them go in one ear and out the other. Some thoughts are happy, and some thoughts are sad. Some thoughts are glad, and some are mad. But we don't hold on to any of them. We let them pass on by just like the clouds in the sky." After that, I have them thank the universe. This can help your anxiety break, even if it's just for a minute. When it does, be grateful. Don't focus on wanting it go away, because it will come back. Just focus on the moment you're in and *right now*. It's OK that you're going through a dark time. Own that shit. Ask for help. You're going to be all right.

Chapter

TWO

WHY THE FUCK VS. WHAT THE FUCK

"He who has a why to live can bear almost any how."
—FRIEDRICH NIETZSCHE

After my breakdown, I realized I had been spending my days ricocheting between ideas of what I needed to "get done." Productivity is positive, but I had neglected to identify the purpose behind my efforts—a dynamic that contributed to the anxiety and sense of fragility that fueled my breakdown.

As I've talked with people facing similar struggles, I found many of those in crisis are asking themselves the wrong questions. You may wake up and wonder, "What am I going to do with my day? My family? My life?" Those are the wrong "w" questions. The real issue isn't *what* you're going to do but *why* you're going to do it. If you want to pull yourself out of depression or anxiety, turn your business around, improve your marriage, or overcome whatever else you're struggling with, *what* you choose to do has to line up with your why.

We live like there will always be a tomorrow, but one day, there won't be. We're all going to die. I'm not suggesting you focus on only that or panic, but it's important to remember our time is limited. Whatever we choose to do with our time here had better be meaningful.

BPP: BEST PARENT POSSIBLE

When I was putting the pieces back together after my breakdown, one of the big issues bothering me was that I didn't have a guiding force in my life. People who are religious have God to dictate what's right and what they should do. If you follow the Bible, you can ask yourself, "What would Jesus do?" I didn't have that.

Before everything came to a head, I had a good material life, but I didn't feel connected to guiding values. I wasn't grounded in any particular belief or mission. I didn't have a good answer to my why. I was struggling with my reason for being here. Eventually, I came to the conclusion that my reason for being was to serve as the best parent possible—BPP. Refocusing myself on parenting helped me orient myself toward my meaning and purpose.

One practice that helps me orient myself this way is my daily meditation practice. Every morning after I meditate, I thank the universe for my children. I start the day by focusing on my love for them and what I want to do for them. I want them to be the best, strongest, most resilient adults they can be. I want them to know how to truly care about people, love people, and accept love in return. I have two sons, and this can be a hard lesson, particularly for males. We're often taught— or, in my case, conditioned—to be so hard and tough that we end up closed off to others. I want something more for my boys.

At the same time, I try to encourage my sons; it's important for me to challenge my kids and help them learn to be resilient through difficult experiences and responsibilities. In middle-class America, I believe many parents have done their children a disservice by making life too easy. Making my kids' lives easier is not on my agenda; I want them to feel committed to putting in the work required to make a family and a household run well. They have chores, even at their young age. I don't set them up for failure, but part of showing them love is challenging them to contribute.

The bottom line? My philosophy of being the BPP isn't to

give my kids the world but rather to equip them to be able to handle the world—and the first and most important part of executing that philosophy is love. How do I do that? I do that by showing them, not telling them, what the best adult looks like. My goal every day is clear: How do I show my kids what it means to be the best adult? The first step of being the best adult, in my opinion, is showing yourself and other people love!

LOVE

You can't be your best self and overcome the challenges you will undoubtedly face in your life if you don't love yourself; this is a crucial part of being the BPP for me. When I was meditating and trying to come to my why, I realized I'd brought two children into the world. How could they *not* be my why? The harder part was figuring out how to do my best for them; I've learned through trial and error, but the key has always been love.

THE BPP LENS

Having my "why" figured out gives me a principle that governs everything I do in life—and not only when my kids are around. How do I act at work? Am I taking time for myself? Everyone needs alone time to recharge, and my kids will need it too as they grow up. Being the BPP is my North Star. In everything I do, I ask myself one question: Is this how I want my children to be or act?

A great example of this principle came up recently when my friend Jay Jack needed a favor. Jay and I started Brazilian Jiu-Jitsu around the same time. He moved to Maine to open his own school when we were purple belts. If you called Jay and told him you accidentally killed someone, he would arrive with a bag, gloves, a shovel, and zero questions. He's just one of those people.

As I've mentioned, much of my anxiety centers on sleep, particularly when I'm traveling. I also hate to travel without my family. When I'm away, I worry about how they're doing and whether I'm going to sleep. A while back, I was traveling all over the place—California to New York to London. I just wanted to be home. Then Jay's wife called. She said he was getting ready to compete again for the first time in ten years, and he needed someone to come train him. Helping him meant I needed to go sleep in some janky hotel in Portland, Maine, away from my family again. Everything in the core of my being didn't want to go. I had just traveled all over the world for the past month. I had spent more time sleeping in a hotel than in my own bed. I just wanted to stay home and get back into my routine. However, I knew what I would want my kids to do for one of their best friends, so on the plane I went.

That doesn't mean it wasn't hard on them. My kids told me they didn't want me to go, but I explained to them I had to because my friend needed my help. Not only was it important for me to be there for him, but it was also important that my kids understood *why* I had to go.

NOT FAKING IT

As I said earlier, I realized that part of being the best parent to my kids meant *showing* them what it looks like to be the best adult possible, not merely telling them what to do without following through myself. Kids listen to your advice for a while, but at a certain point, they'll rebel. As the saying goes, the world is changed by your example, not your opinion.

I model hard work for them. My businesses are set up in such a way that I don't have to work as much as I do, but hard work is how I got where I am, so I keep it up. My work is also something I love—it aligns with my why—and I'm modeling the importance of that alignment too. I want my kids to see you can't reach your full potential going to a job you hate every day.

I also do my very best to treat my wife well all the time, not just when the kids are watching. I'm modeling for them how to treat a spouse, and I can't slip up. My wife and I don't reinforce conventional gender roles. I cook and clean. She fixes things around the house. My kids see that we each do what needs to be done.

In addition, I demonstrate love for my friends. I don't just *like* my friends—I *love* them. I want my kids to understand the love that goes into real friendship. I don't tell them one thing but do another. I *show* them how to be a true friend.

I've learned that when it comes to teaching your kids, you can't fake it. The real you will shine through. They see you every day, including your worst moments. They will understand your true character. Unfortunately, it's human nature to remember the worst about people, not always the best. For my boys, I want to be the best I can be, even in my worst moments. For me, being the BPP means giving my all—and saying sorry quickly when I falter.

IT'S NOT ABOUT BEING RIGHT

Being right is not part of being the BPP. Fuck being right. I used to (and still do) struggle with having to be right all the time. I'd argue everything to death. Then I realized even when I'm "right," I'm not necessarily right. Right is often relative. Certain things are objectively true, like the sun rising in the morning, but much of being right is just about my subjective narrative.

For example, I've learned a lot from having millennials,

who grew up in the generation after mine, as employees. I was raised by people who experienced racial prejudice and survived the Holocaust. My attitude has been to do what I'm told and get my work done; by and large, they were raised differently. I used to get frustrated when my millennial employees weren't getting their work done. I can't tell you how many people I've called into my office, thinking they were lazy or not moving fast enough.

Then I got better at understanding their point of view. Everyone is capable of hard work. It's not that millennials refuse to work, but in my experience, they don't blindly do what they're told. They want to know why they're being asked to do something and what the point is. Their generation actually has that right: they put a greater emphasis on their why.

I'm a business owner and I have to focus on productivity. I used to think my way was not just the right way but the *only* way for the business to move forward. Now I've let go of that attitude. Objectively, my way was not the only right way just because it's what came to my mind first. Working with younger employees forced me to open up to the multiple possible ways of getting things done. When I changed my approach and asked them how they would like to complete tasks—and I actually took their feedback into account—we arrived at a place of mutual understanding that benefited my business. I began to see much better production from my employees—a shift that, again, flowed from my commitment to being the BPP.

Sometimes we don't see there's more than one way to live our lives, and we can get stuck in our ways and rigid in our attitudes. When I found my why, I could see more clearly and think more expansively. My children were a big part of this realization; I have two little boys who live in the same household but have their own distinct personalities, neither right nor wrong. And guess what? I raised both of them. Nobody else touched them but me and my wife, and even so, they approach their lives differently and as unique individuals. In trying to be the BPP, I know I need to talk to them differently to achieve the same results. That experience has helped me deal with everyone in my life more effectively.

FINDING YOUR WHY

Finding your purpose isn't a simple task; entire books have been written on the subject, so don't worry if yours doesn't come to you right away. My why is being the BPP. Some of the steps I took to find mine were meditation, journaling, applying the principle of extreme ownership, and going to therapy.

MEDITATION

If you're in a rough spot, get through that fire first; remember, do *right now*, over and over. Then you can focus on the bigger questions and finding your why. Meditating can help you get there. I came to meditation because, while I knew we all needed something to guide us in our lives, mainstream religion never worked for me. I didn't want a kind of spirituality that forced me to believe things I didn't actually believe. I found my way to Stoicism, and a central aspect of Stoic philosophy is meditation.

Meditation is my time with my version of God. When I meditate, I have time with whatever created the universe; it's just the two of us. There's nothing else going on during that time. In its truest form, meditation is simply being intentionally still for ten minutes a day. When people tell me they don't have ten minutes to meditate and be with themselves, I tell them they must need an hour. *Everyone* can find ten minutes.

I've been meditating for about three years now. I go to a room by myself and shut the door. I started the practice when my youngest son was two. He's five now, and he knows the drill—when the door is closed, Daddy's off limits. I do a guided meditation because it helps me stay in the moment and focus on my breath. That's all you want to do when you meditate—you're not "doing nothing." Instead, you're focusing on your breath going in and out. Personally, I lie down and feel the pressure of my back on the floor, and noticing what's in the moment. When I'm finished meditating, I thank the universe—for everything, including my problems, because they're what will make me great.

When I first started meditating, I was terrible at it, and that's OK. Everyone is terrible at it in the beginning! When you try it, your thoughts will come and go. Maybe you start following one thought, and another one pops up. You may get frustrated and think to yourself, *Shit. I'm supposed to be meditating.* Guess what? You already are. If you feel this way, simply bring your attention back to your breath and the present moment. Try to focus on each breath in its entirety and then the next. See how many you can do without getting sidetracked on another thought; I challenge you to get to five breaths. The most experienced meditators can get to five or ten.

In the end, meditation is a form of surrender that gives you more power in the rest of your life—power you can use to find your why.

JOURNALING

When you're in the pits of an anxiety-induced hell, your first priority is getting out. That's the kind of situation for the "what if" journaling I described earlier. If you're in hell, you have to figure out how to deal with that suffering first. When you begin to improve, the principle of journaling is still the same: write down whatever you're thinking. It's that simple and that important. Just get the thoughts out of your head and onto paper so that you don't let them spin around all day.

In my case, whatever I wrote down ended up linking back to my kids, and that helped me arrive at trying to be the BPP. There's no rule, though. Write whatever is going through your mind. Getting out what's bothering you can help you gain perspective and clarity.

EXTREME OWNERSHIP

Jocko Willink, ex-Navy SEAL and author of *Extreme Ownership*, provides a great example for finding your why. Willink was part of the first cohort to see combat again after our country had a long period without war or troops on the ground. In the time without military conflict, many experienced veterans had retired or died, so war became just an idea, in a way. Fighting strategies and tactics were based on theory rather than real-life experience, which was problematic. Think about it: when you go into battle, you want to know how people have succeeded in the past.

Jocko was in the first wave of soldiers to see actual wartime again, and it was tough. He and his fellow troop members had to figure out a lot of things on the fly. They'd try what they were taught and realize, *Oh, shit. That didn't work.* Through his experiences as a SEAL, he came to the concept of extreme ownership.

Extreme ownership says every single thing in your life is your responsibility. All the bad shit that happens in your life isn't *done* to you; it *belongs* to you. The concept is beautiful, because if your problems belong to you—if they're your fault—they can actually be fixed. You can't resolve your issues if they are somebody else's responsibility. Taking ownership of your life is another form of Stoic philosophy; control what you can control. When you do, you have all the power.

The concept of extreme ownership has been revolutionary in my recovery and my life. I had to take full control. In finding my why, I realized nobody gets to have my day. If my wife is taking her frustration out on me, for example, I can choose my reaction. Everyone has bad days—myself included—so there is no blame to place. However, the way I proceed to deal with the situation is my choice. Any frustration I have as a result is on me. My anger is mine; others do not cause it. My pain is mine; others do not cause it. By taking that perspective, not only can I handle any situation, but I can also change it for the better. Once you take extreme ownership, you can see your place in the world and find out why you exist.

THERAPY

A woman I worked with, Ellie, came to me with some of the same problems I'd experienced. She wasn't sleeping. She was racked with anxiety. I wanted to help her get to the why questions, but I knew I had to start with what to open up that dialogue.

"What do you think is causing your struggle right now?" I asked.

She said she didn't know. All she felt was that she didn't know where her life was going and that she didn't have any answers.

I told her what I tell a lot of people in her situation—first, that I understood. Then something else.

"Let me ask you this," I said. "Are you going to die in this moment? Like, right now?"

"No, of course not," she said.

"OK, great," I told her. "I only need you to do right now. Let's just take this moment to moment."

Sometimes I find people like Ellie tell me that the moment-to-moment approach is fine during the day, but the problem really rears its head at night. They can't sleep. Everyone is asleep except for them, and they panic. They feel like they're going crazy. Having suffered from insomnia in the past, I understand.

I got a call the other night from someone in that mindset, and I told him staying in bed and doing nothing wasn't going to solve anything. I reminded him he needed something to do with his spinning mind and told him to find something to watch on Netflix. Not only that, but I also had him send me a screenshot to prove it. Without accountability, it's too easy to say you're going to do something and not follow through, especially when you're in hell.

I tell people going through a rough period that they can call me anytime. Often, they call and tell me they found a solution to their issue. They're excited, and I tell them I'm happy for them, knowing they didn't actually find the magic answer. Still, looking for solutions is the first step. They're getting somewhere. Without the anchor of the why though, it can all fall apart easily.

For example, Ellie thought she'd solved her problem— only to call me a couple of mornings later in a panic because her plan didn't work.

"Fuck, fuck," she repeated into the phone.

"OK," I said. "The plan you thought was going to get you

out of this just failed. That's OK. Here is the advice my wife gave me: go through the day as you would if you had gotten sleep. Just do today."

Then I began talking to Ellie about some of her big-picture issues. She was in her early twenties, trying to figure out what to make of her life. It felt overwhelming. As I talked more deeply with her about her problems and what she felt her purpose was, I suggested she go to therapy. Initially, she was resistant.

Then I asked her the question that has worked on everyone I've encountered so far: "Do you brush your teeth every day?"

"What the fuck does that have to do with anything?" she asked. I told her just to answer the question.

"Yes," she said.

"Do you brush your teeth even when your teeth are falling out?" I asked her.

"No, I brush them so that they *don't* fall out," she said.

"Exactly," I told her. "That's why you need to go to therapy."

People go to therapy in a crisis, and then as soon as

they start to feel a little better, they stop going. Therapy is there to help prevent crises, though. When you're feeling better, you keep going. You can go to the dentist when your teeth are rotted out and get a whole new set of fake teeth, or you can follow the dentist's advice and brush your teeth every day to prevent the rot in the first place. I told Ellie she needed to brush her teeth twice a day, every day—and tend to her emotional health too.

Therapy is necessary preventive life care. Some people have a skewed perception of what therapy is or what it's for. They think it isn't for them. In reality, it's basic care. It's essential.

In Ellie's case, she found a therapist who could start helping her work through her confusion. Eventually, they were able to discuss not only what was wrong, but what was right, too. She realized what made her happy was traveling and being exposed to different cultures, because those experiences had made her more empathetic and open to people. She decided she wanted to give back to others. She discovered her passion, her why. So she opened her own business to expose young people to different cultures.

Her new situation isn't always easy. Sometimes, she has to work long hours and still struggles to pay her bills.

However, her entire attitude has changed, because she now has her why.

Bottom line: when you figure out your purpose in life, you're fine, even when it's difficult. When you're not aligned with your "why," it's all too easy not to feel OK.

NEVER DONE

Finding your purpose doesn't mean you'll never be fatigued again. If you feel committed to what you're doing, though, the hard work doesn't faze you as much. You might have to go to bed at midnight and wake up at 4:00 a.m. You're not sleeping much, but it's a good kind of not sleeping. It's similar to staying up with a sick child; that kind of loss of sleep doesn't faze you because you love your kid so much.

Never being done is actually the most beautiful part about finding your why. In my case, what it means to be the BPP will constantly change. Being the best parent today is different from being the best parent when my kids are eighteen, twenty-five, or forty-five. I hope to stay healthy so that I can keep striving toward my why for the rest of my life. When I close my eyes for the last time, I want the sense of peace that will come from knowing my life was oriented toward a greater purpose. I want to be able to say I lived every day with true meaning. Not the superficial type of meaning that comes from the kind of car I drive, or any of the other material things I might get wrapped up in day to day either, but from asking much deeper, more important questions.

Let me be clear: finding your why doesn't mean you'll have smooth sailing from here on out. Living with purpose is hard. It's challenging. Nothing you hold special in your heart was easily gained. When things are easy, you forget about them. They don't mean a thing. It's getting through the hard shit that gives you a sense of pride. I love my kids so much *because* raising them is fucking hard, but they're worth it.

Being the BPP is my why. What's yours?

Chapter

THREE

MY OBSTACLES SHOW ME THE WAY

"The impediment to action advances action.
What stands in the way becomes the way."

—MARCUS AURELIUS

I'm not religious, so I call Michael A. Singer's *The Untethered Soul* my Old Testament and Ryan Holiday's *The Obstacle Is the Way* my New Testament. Holiday's book, in particular, changed my life. It was where I first encountered the quote above, which I now have tattooed on my arm in Greek.

That quote impacted me because it made me realize everything I felt was stopping me was actually doing the opposite. Instead, it was showing me the action I had to take. Those words led to my aha, godlike moment. I'm now more focused on the idea of something greater than me. I talk to the universe and thank God every day. I don't know what or who that is, but I'm not concerned about it either. I am able to say thank you for the challenges and opportunities in my life.

Holiday's book truly showed me that what stands in the way becomes the way. All my obstacles are there to show me the way. Nowhere has this been more obvious in my life than during my time in the UFC.

MAKING MY WAY IN THE UFC

Let me be clear: I signed up for the UFC and knew what I was getting into, so I don't place any blame on them. Still, it was brutal and ruthless—and I'm not just talking about the cage.

Here's how the UFC works: if you win and you're exciting to watch, you stay. That's it. There's not much care for the fighters, especially the ones who aren't at the top. Nowhere is this truer than when it comes to finances. When I was in the league, fighters made 8 percent of the total revenue. The top ten fighters made 7 percent of that figure, and the remaining 1 percent was split among all 290 guys on the roster. It's different than in other sports, where 50 percent of the revenue that comes in is distributed to the players. In the NFL, for example, the Tom

Bradys and Peyton Mannings of the world are going to make more of that 50 percent than the third-string quarterback who never sees action. Still, that third-string quarterback is going to be a millionaire too.

Not in the UFC. It's all about the bottom line.

I won three fights in the UFC. Even though I was winning, I wasn't serving that bottom line very well because I wasn't the most exciting fighter to watch. I wasn't going to live and die on the sword. Why do you think people liked to watch Mike Tyson or Manny Pacquiao fight so much? Because there was a possibility somebody could die. The crowd wants someone to be knocked out. They want blood. I fought more like Floyd Mayweather, without the undefeated record: I was deliberate. I outpointed people. I wasn't all that promotable.

Fighting in the UFC is like Russian roulette. At every point, every fighter is worried about their money and their job. If they win, their pay doubles. If they lose, they could be out. There's no guarantee beyond one fight at a time.

At twenty-nine, I found myself on the chopping block after a bad fight. My time in the UFC was about to run out.

GETTING CUT

I had won three matches in the UFC, and I was preparing for my fourth fight. The eight-week training camp had started one month after my son was born. If you're a parent, you know that's a rough time of life; among other things, I was sleep-deprived.

When fight day came, I didn't perform my best. I didn't get beat up, but I didn't kick ass either. In the end, I lost by split decision: two of the judges had called it for my opponent, and one had called it for me. Still, I had a winning record overall, and I was hopeful my place might still be there. The next morning, though, I got a call saying I was released.

I was devastated. My dream was crushed, and I cried afterward. I'd just gone through an extensive training camp leading up to a fifteen-minute fight. For two months, my whole life had revolved around preparing for that tiny period of time, and I lost. I felt like a failure and like less of a man. All I could see was that I'd made only half the money I could have made in the fight, and then I was released—with a wife on maternity leave and new baby at home. What was I going to do?

MINOR LEAGUE

I decided to go straight into fighting in the minor league

because it was my only chance to stay on the UFC's radar. I agreed to two fights with less than two weeks between them—not something you do for a key reason: fights are grueling.

Even in a fight you win (unless it's under a minute), somebody kicked you and punched you in the head. And the shots that don't win fights—the ones you simply have to block and defend against with nothing but your body—are still brutal. It's the nature of the beast.

I had a rough time when I entered the minor league for these reasons and then some. In my first fight, I got kicked in the groin, which is illegal. I still won the fight, but my testicle had gotten squished between the edge of my steel cup and my leg. It swelled to the size of a baseball, and I had another fight scheduled twelve days later. In between the fights, not only could I barely walk—let alone train— but I also essentially couldn't eat in order to make weight. I took the fight anyway, and I won that one too.

Then, about two months later, an opportunity came up to fight in the Dominican Republic. The pay was really good: fifteen thousand dollars compared to the $2,000 per fight I'd been making since I'd gotten cut. It was like UFC pay without being in the UFC, but it was risky. Unlike in the United States, which has a commission to make sure the rules are followed and the money is there, there aren't any protections to speak of for the fighters in other countries. But I needed the money.

I traveled to the Dominican Republic two weeks before Christmas for the fight, and immediately upon arriving, I realized it was a total shit show. When it was time to weigh in, for example, the organizers had all the fighters wait for the "official scale." In the States, the official scale is a badass, perfectly calibrated setup that gets your weight perfectly dialed in. In this instance, though, the organizers brought in a regular digital scale from one of the bathrooms of the hotel we were staying in. I thought, *Are you fucking serious?*

The "arena" was the auditorium of a middle school, a place where twelve-year-olds do talent shows. There were maybe fifteen people in the room other than the fighters, and I was used to fighting in front of five thousand to ten thousand spectators. The other fighters and I sat on the stage, awaiting our turn.

Normally, fights are three five-minute rounds, but the first round of the first fight went on for eight minutes because they didn't have a timer. In the second round, one of the fighters got brutally knocked out—and only then did we learn there was no doctor. It's a big enough risk just to fight, but usually there's a doctor and an ambulance to take you away if necessary. In the United States, again, the commission ensures safeguards like that for the fighter. Not there.

Holy fuck, this is terrible, I thought. *I've got to do this fast. Time to change my fighting style: blood and guts. I need to finish this fight quickly.*

I got the takedown and then quickly worked to the submission—got it done in two minutes! I collected my check, went back to my hotel, and flew home the next day. When I got back to the United States, the $15,000 check bounced. To add insult to injury, I'd turned down a $6,000 fight to take the one in the Dominican Republic. I looked at my situation: I'd risked my life for this fight. I was no longer making any money from the UFC. Christmas was coming, and now I had nothing.

I was down, but I wasn't out.

Two months later, I got a call from the UFC. It turned out someone had fallen off the roster, and they wanted me to step in for a fight—with ten days' notice. I had another chance, and I took it.

I'd like this to be the part of the story where I ride off into the sunset, but that's not how it happened. Ten days wasn't enough time to prepare, and I got destroyed.

THE MENTAL SIDE OF FIGHTING

Fighting is difficult because it's super-raw and all-consuming. When you fight for a living, you have to dedicate your whole life to it. The average number of events is three fifteen-minute fights per year, so fighters dedicate their lives to what amounts to less than one hour in the cage per year. Under those circumstances, you can't have a bad day at work. There isn't room for it. The job is the definition of pressure.

If you win, you always fight somebody better. It's not like the NFL schedule where there are weeks you're playing a weak team. In the UFC, the risks get higher, the fights get harder, and the potential purse grows with each fight.

Fighting is also different from other leagues, because when you step into the cage, you're on your own. You might train with a fantastic team, but when it comes to the fight, everything rests on you. Your true character can't help but come out, and whatever is going on in your life will affect you.

Then, if you get cut, all that—all you've worked for—comes to an abrupt halt.

When they get cut, some fighters get depressed and take time off. I didn't do that. I went straight into the minor league fights. Although my ego was bruised, that's what pushed me forward. Eventually, though, I realized that when I was on the big stage, my standards for myself hadn't been high enough. And my settling had been partly what led to my being cut in the first place. Yes, I'd worked really hard—no one outworks me, ever, even to this day—but at the same time, I was stubborn about my fighting style. *I'm winning this way*, I told myself. *Why would I change?* I completely missed the fact that my relatively boring, strategic style opened me up to getting cut after one loss. When that time came, because I'd been resting on my laurels and relying on one way of fighting, the UFC had one thing to say: OK, bye.

I felt broken down during that period, but I didn't give up. That same mentality that helped me fight my way back into the league is also what helped me after my breakdown.

LEARNING TO KEEP FIGHTING

One of my favorite quotes from *Fight Club* is, "After fighting, everything else in your life got the volume turned down." Nothing else is as intense as the time in the cage; the only comparable experience I've had, in fact, is the panic and anxiety I went through a couple of years later. Facing that intensity both in the cage and in my life taught me a simple truth: life sucks sometimes. There's no way around it. What matters is what you do in those dark times.

One of my friends once told me, "Bro, you're not a fighter until you've lost a fight and then fight again, because who can't ride the bandwagon?" He's right. It's easy to roll with the momentum when you're smashing everybody. In the beginning, good fighters start out beating everyone. They don't fucking lose. They go out there in the cage time and time again, and it's a party. It's like childhood: a good childhood starts out easy, and your parents protect you. At some point, though, you're a teenager and you start having to rely on yourself and face challenges without them. You lose a fight here or there. If you don't lay good groundwork in the beginning, those transitional moments—those challenges, those losses—can break you.

Fighting taught me how to get through difficult times in my life. I had to learn how to assess everything objectively and not let my emotions get ahead of me. I had to learn to get some distance from my feelings. Why? If you fight *purely* from raw emotion, that might serve you well for a time, but at some point, it will bite you in the ass. If you're all emotion and don't keep your head in the game, you might win your first ten fights or overcome a string of key challenges. But what happens in the third round of your eleventh fight? What happens when you're exhausted and you've used up everything you had? You're not even going to be able to keep your hands up if you don't pace yourself and balance your emotion with your physical ability.

Fighting taught me that uncontrollably burning through your energy (both physical and mental energy) can destroy you. You have to learn to exercise control. If your opponent punches you hard, the next second may or may not be the time to punch him back. You might have to just eat that punch for a minute, get your shit together, and then get him. You might have to strategize and go in a little later instead of reacting immediately. It's the same in life.

BE GRATEFUL FOR EVERY BATTLE YOU GET TO HAVE

Life is hard, but we are lucky to get to have problems. They mean you're still alive and fighting for something. If you're not fighting, you're either living a terrible, boring life doing nothing, or you're dead. I choose neither. Death is coming for me. I can't do anything about that. But while I'm alive, I say this: *bring on all the problems you've got. What do you have today for me, Universe? I'm ready.*

Is this mentality easy? No. Just when you think you've got it figured out, what happens? You get kicked. You're about to win the fight, and then boom: you get caught with a shot you didn't see coming. All right. Word. Let's go.

In work, marriage, parenting, meeting your personal goals—any of it—terrible things are *going* to happen. You won't like it. You don't want to get hit with that shot, but you have no choice. In those moments, you have two options: you can complain about it and express your disbelief about being unlucky, or you can face it and work through your shit. It won't be easy or fun, but in the end, pushing through and growing from those experiences is the way forward.

When I took that first minor league fight, I literally got kicked in the nuts. I don't think my opponent did that intentionally, but that doesn't change the outcome: cheap shot or not, I had to deal with it. My reaction and next steps were my responsibility. We worry too often about whether things are fair. Tell me, when was the last time life was really fair? Is it fair somebody else gets a job you deserved? Is it fair your spouse cheats on you? Go further: Is it fair to be born in sub-Saharan Africa with no running water? Is it fair to grow up homeless because your parents are addicted to drugs? No. None of that is fucking fair. We can argue the fair thing all day long, but my point is that it's the *wrong question*. It's not about what is fair; it's about what you're going to do next.

DBAB: DON'T BE A BITCH OR A BULLY

First, let's be clear. Being a bitch has nothing at all to do with the female gender. Anyone can be a bitch. A bitch is someone who allows their problems, their weaknesses, their struggles, and their fears to halt them. This is not to say that *having* problems, weakness, struggles, and fear makes you a bitch; it makes you the opposite. Having them makes you human. Letting them halt you makes you a bitch.

DBAB means Don't Be a Bitch, but it also means Don't Be a Bully. They're two sides of the same coin. Sometimes, when we're struggling, we try to place blame or shift our struggle onto other people. We try to bully them and make them feel like we're feeling. A bully, in this sense, is anyone who realizes their fear and uses it to put down other people. To shame them. To hurt them. You can't be a bully without being a bitch.

You've got to DBAB at both ends of the spectrum: when life is going well and when it's hard. Whether you're faced with fear or you're in a good spot, you can't be a bitch and you can't be a bully. DBAB. Have the tough conversations, with yourself or with others. Show up and show love. Don't project your shit on other people or let it hold you down. Be honest. Move on. Wake up, meditate, thank the universe, and realize the obstacle is the way. Then DBAB every single day!

TOUGH BUT RESPECTFUL CONVERSATIONS

How, exactly, do you DBAB? It starts with tough but respectful conversations. We often run away from these types of conversations with ourselves and with others. We don't like to have them. They're uncomfortable.

We often avoid such confrontations because, at first, it's easier just to keep things right where they are. When we don't deal with issues right away, it's *possible* that problems might improve on their own, but it's not probable. Usually, things stay the same. Speaking directly and respectfully, though, can lead to true progress.

One of the biggest components of being a bitch or a bully is not showing love to people, which is especially common among young males. Men in particular often feel scared to express their emotions. You might think demonstrating love makes you look weak, but it's the opposite. You've had your heart broken? Good. It sucks. I get it. Now go do it again. Real love requires the strength to keep being there for people.

If people love each other, they stick around for the bad times. I don't love my wife just for all the good times we've had—I have good times with a lot of people. I love my wife because it's shitty sometimes and she's still here. We might stay up four nights in a row with the kids and both be wrecked. Then we get up and do it again. That's what love is: sticking together to push through the hard times.

In *Good Will Hunting*, Robin Williams's character tells

Matt Damon that his wife used to fart. It smelled so bad it would wake both of them and the dog up in the middle of the night. He didn't have the heart to tell her it was her. He always said it was the dog. That's what love is. His wife had died in the movie, and he said what he missed the most were the little things no one else knew about, because they were for him. The rest of the world gets our public persona. We can't help it. People put makeup on and make themselves look nice to go out, but what do you look like in the morning? Nothing. Bad breath, messy hair, smelly farts. The people who matter love us *because* of who we are naturally. That's what true love is. Valuing the people around you in the same way is what true DBAB'ing is.

THE GIFT OF PRESSURE

The love we give might not be returned at some points. Sometimes, in fact, the person we love might put pressure on us that we don't like. Pressure, just like problems, is a gift. When you see a hard situation as a gift, you can embrace it rather than crumble under the weight of it.

We got here as human beings through pressure. We evolved from a single-celled organism, thanks to the pressure put on us by the universe and the earth. The single cell continued changing and getting better. A couple of million years later, here we are. I don't know what comes next, but whatever we become as a species will result from the pressure applied to us.

Our lives are what they are *because* of pressure. Why do we have houses? We needed shelter to survive. Why do we form families? We found they're the best way to raise a human being, a small child.

Bottom line: we can't avoid pressure; we have to prepare for it. We all have to do hard shit. How? I recommend working out intensely, especially when you're struggling. You'll feel better by accomplishing something. You'll be ready for the next time that something feels difficult. Personally, I draw on the strength from my fighting days *because* it was hard. I lean on my grandparents' example *because* they made it through. I know I can handle whatever comes my way.

Do things that are going to push you. You'll build self-esteem by shattering your own expectations. If you're coasting, how will you have anything to fall back on when you need to believe in yourself? Run toward the pressure, not away from it.

BPP AND PRESSURE ON KIDS

Pressure is a gift that you should give children too. I have a job. My wife has a job. We're both educated, and we come from educated households. My kids are lucky. As part of my BPP mission, my job is to make their lives harder. Too often, we think, *I want my kids to have a better life than I did.* It's true that I want my children to have a better life than I did, but the way I'm going to do that is by showing them what struggle looks like.

Being loving, caring, and nurturing are essential to good parenting. What else is? Letting your kids fail. Their failure is not your failure. Tell them the score even if they lost. Let them know how they rank in their class at school. Give them work to do that is challenging.

In my house, we give our kids jobs. Unfortunately, it's harder for us at first than it would be if we just did the tasks ourselves. For example, my kids have been unloading the dishwasher since my youngest was three years old. At first, some dishes were broken and messes were made, but they learned. Today, they feel pride in themselves because they can handle responsibilities that help the whole family.

My oldest son also cuts the grass. I used to cut the grass as a kid myself, and my dad would always come check to see if I did it right. I *always* missed a spot. I still remember the very first time he didn't check. I was so proud. I knew he trusted my ability, and he didn't even have to say anything.

My oldest has had that experience too. He's been cutting the grass for two years now. At first, he couldn't even start the lawn mower. He missed spots all over. Now I'm about to buy him a new mower, and he's excited. He's earned it.

His pride came through pressure. Through crying. Through failure.

"Dad, I can't cut the grass right," he used to tell me, tearfully.

"I know, buddy," I'd say. "You sure didn't cut the grass right, but there's only one way to learn. So go cut the grass."

The gift of pressure and the importance of extreme ownership go hand in hand, and my sons are learning them from me every day. It's part of being the BPP.

BE SCARED AND DO IT ANYWAY

Burt Watson, whom I mentioned earlier as the granddaddy of the UFC, started out as manager for Joe Frazier, boxing heavyweight champion of the world. He's not with the UFC anymore, but we used to call him the babysitter to the stars. He took care of us during fight week. He checked us in and made us feel like a million bucks. He'd been in the business forever and knew exactly how we felt. He'd get us amped up and call on us to "roll to the hole."

When you heard that—oh, fuck. Your whole body would tense, but you had to walk. He would walk every single one of us all the way down to that cage. He was just doing his job, but the way he treated us helped us get over our fear. It helped us move forward. We were scared, but we did it anyway. That's a lesson I have for my children.

Our job as humans is to embrace the obstacles before us. To roll to the hole every time. To look fear in the face and say, "Not today." For example, I'm competing again to raise money for charity and also because I want to lead by example. I want my sons to see me on the days of my competitions, feeling scared and nervous. I could so easily focus on what I accomplished in the past and rest on my laurels. My kids love to look at my medals, trophies, and belts. Those are great, but they all represent the past. I did that already. It's OK to have scared days because we do scared days too. That's how it rolls.

Continuing to compete is risky for me and my business. I'm one of the few martial arts school owners who still fights. If I lose, it could negatively affect my bottom line. At the end of the day, though, fear of losing students because of losing a competition is one of those anxiety-producing what-ifs. In spite of my fears, I have to go out there and compete anyway.

For you, feeling scared and doing it anyway might not be

about competition. Maybe, like so many people, you're looking for a real relationship. You might be tempted to play it safe by using dating apps, and meeting people for only happy hour or coffee. Fuck that. Put yourself out there. Have a whole dinner. Let the other person get to know you and get to know them too. It might suck, but take the risk anyway. Don't let yourself bail after a ten-minute coffee date. Go in with the expectation that you'll stay for two hours. Give the other person a chance. Actually try to connect. The scary part isn't that you might not like the other person or waste your time—it's opening yourself up and letting yourself be fully seen, flaws and all. It's not easy. Do it anyway.

EMBRACING YOUR FEAR

What are *you* most afraid of? What petrifies you?

Something that still petrifies me every night is whether or not I'll get to sleep. I still wonder whether tonight will mark the beginning of never sleeping again. I start with acceptance, telling myself I'm going to stay up all night and watch TV. Then I turn on a show that's monotonous, and I tell myself I'm going to watch it. Eventually, I start to get a little tired and find myself fighting to stay awake. During the commercial break, I tell myself I'll just close my eyes for a minute, but I have to open them again when the show comes back on. Pretty soon, I can't keep my eyes open, and I tell myself I'm just going to listen to the story. Then I fully fall asleep.

Your fear might not be insomnia and all that comes with it. It could be and probably is very different. The message here, however, is the same: whatever you're afraid of in your life, go tackle it. When you're facing down your fear and your whole body tenses up, remember Burt Watson. "It's time to roll to the hole, baby!"

Let's go.

Chapter FOUR

SCREAM YOUR WEAKNESSES TO THE WORLD

"Courage starts with showing up and letting ourselves be seen."
—BRENÉ BROWN

I know I'm a role model in the martial arts community because I've been successful. Some people think I have it all: I've fought in the UFC and I've been a Brazilian Jiu-Jitsu champion. I own multiple successful martial arts schools. It's human nature to put people up on pedestals. We think if we could just get to where someone else is, our problems would go away. But that's not how it works.

On the day of my last fight, I was crying in my hotel room.

I told my wife I was so fucking scared, and I was. That was the first time I ever truly told someone how I was feeling in a moment when I was vulnerable. It's easy to express anger. People can see when you're mad at them. When we're afraid, though, we usually try to hide it. Being honest with my wife was the first time I admitted my fear as an adult.

I couldn't get out of my last fight, though. I'd never been so scared in my life. Fighting is scary in general, and there are so many unknowns. You're wondering, *What will happen to me? Will I be alive after this confrontation that for some dumb reason I'm agreeing to have?*

For me, the fact I had done poorly in my previous fight compounded my usual fears. I'd quit that fight mentally, and I wondered if I'd do so again. I couldn't get away from the what-ifs. Finally, I spoke to Renee. My wife is my world, and that moment was my first time screaming my weakness to the world. It was a game changer.

When we're kids, we scream our weakness all the time. Babies cry whenever they need something. Young children say, "Mommy and Daddy, I'm scared of the dark." It's simply natural. Then, at some point, we stop verbalizing what we're feeling and what we need. We realize we have to start taking care of ourselves, and we come to believe that we can't tell the world everything.

In adulthood, some of us take that independenc and we hold everything in. We decide not to say to anybody. We pretend we're always fine. Eve time I had anxiety fifteen years ago, I told a few people, but I was really hush-hush about it. I made the few people I did tell swear not to tell anyone. When my friends would ask why I wasn't drinking with them, I'd lie and say I was allergic to alcohol. The truth was, I knew the feeling of being drunk could trigger my anxiety. Instead of telling more than a handful of people, though, I'd lie to get out of situations.

The more distance we put between us and those around us, the more people feel like they can't achieve what we've achieved—which is the opposite of what I want to teach and what I believe. There's nothing special about me. Today, I find talking about our weaknesses is even more important than talking about strengths. Yes, there are unique skills I have and accomplishments I've made, but I don't have it all. I have flaws. I have struggles. We're all in the same boat.

The more we can pick each other up, the better life will be for everyone. We have to start with our own communities, neighborhoods, school districts, and workplaces. If somebody approaches you and says, "You don't understand what it's like to be me," you shouldn't change the subject. Instead, with pure sincerity, say, "My man, tell me what it's like to be you." Then shut the fuck up and listen. When they're done, say, "Me too, bro. Thanks for sharing."

Letting go of your ego and listening instead of arguing will help you truly understand the other person. They, in turn, will feel heard and lower their walls. Men in particular deal with emotions and ego fueled by testosterone. They suffer from not knowing how to be vulnerable with one another. Men often achieve career success by being able to put their emotions aside and grind through their work.

There has to be room for weakness, and you have to be able to quiet down your ego. Breaking down our egos allows us to see that we give ourselves the best possibility for success and happiness when we do things together. No one fights a war alone. Why fight life alone? We can get everyone on the same train and tackle life together.

SCREAMING MY WEAKNESSES TO HELP OTHERS

I had my most recent breakdown on a Friday. Saturday night, fresh on some medicine, I slept. Then I got all wrapped up in my head. I convinced myself the sleeping pills wouldn't work. I didn't sleep at all Sunday night. When Monday hit, I was in a panic. I felt like the devil had ahold of me.

My wife was at work and my kids were at school. On my

way to my martial arts school, I broke down. I realized I couldn't go inside the building, so I went to my sister-in-law's house a few miles from my business. She put a movie on for her oldest, held her baby, and sat with me while I cried. When the episode finally passed, I went to work, but the problems only continued.

When I reached work, I started talking to my great friend Ian, who's one of my general managers. I was supposed to teach a class, but I started crying again. It was craziness. I don't know what state my brain was in at the time, but I do know what I was thinking: *Fuck, I can't do this. I'm going home.*

I didn't think I could lead my class. I had to leave. I looked outside, though, and realized I needed a new plan. It was rush hour and the traffic was mayhem. It was clear I was either going to sit in gridlock and have a breakdown, or teach and have a breakdown. *Fine,* I thought, *I'll teach.*

The devil still had me. I looked still, but my muscles felt like they were shaking from the inside. It felt like they might explode out of my skin or become paralyzed, so I couldn't move. I couldn't regulate my body temperature. One minute, I was freezing, and the next, I was dumping sweat. It felt like having a fever. I wasn't actually sick, but my body was reacting like I was.

The cause of these symptoms is the stress hormone, cortisol, pumping through the body. I felt like I was losing control. Like every vicious thing in the world was going to take me somewhere and torture me while I was fully conscious the whole time. When the devil gets ahold of you like that, sometimes it feels like it would be better if you died. I wasn't depressed when I went through all these feelings; I was just so fucking afraid.

Somehow, though, I got out of my office and taught the class. Ian watched in case he needed to take over. He didn't tell me that was what he was doing, but I knew he was there if I needed him.

It may sound strange, but getting in front of the class calmed me down. Maybe even more than being a good dad, teaching and connecting with students are what I do best.

MAKING A CONNECTION

At the end of every class I teach, I like to talk a little bit and pass along some inspiration. My students knew about my anxiety; I'd been pretty open about having it in my rearview mirror. On this particular day, though, I thought it would be powerful to talk about what I was going through *in that moment*. The worst part about anxiety can be feeling alone. Knowing someone else is struggling with the same thing can make you feel a little better. I figured somebody else might be doing badly right then too.

I stood on the cage and called all the classes around me to come together. As around one hundred students gathered, I told them everything: That the struggles I'd had in the past were back. That I was in a terrible spot but would be OK. That I wasn't telling them for sympathy; I wanted them to know they weren't alone.

Me? The leader of the school? The strong guy who fought in the UFC? The one whose medals were all over the school? My message was clear: *Yeah, guys. Me too.*

After I spoke, the group was quiet. Some people came up and gave me a hug. Some people put their hands together like they were praying and nodded toward me to say thank you. It was remarkable.

Since that day, communication and connection in the academy have been much better, and so have I. Everyone lowered their walls a little bit after that, and they've kept them down. They've stopped feeling the need to protect themselves so much from other people really knowing them.

Colleges today have "safe spaces" where you're not supposed to have to hear anything you don't want to hear.

That kind of avoidance doesn't solve problems; it makes everyone weaker. I believe a real safe space is where you can feel comfortable *and* have pressure applied to you. Don't get me wrong: it's not that no one will ever say something that offends you. In fact, something offensive is likely to be said to you—not to mention the fact that someone is going to try to choke you unconscious. But we'll try to teach you how to deal with both.

When you show people the real you, you make a connection. Then your situation becomes more of a "we" than an "I." When I was honest with my students about how I was doing, they approached me and told me they were there for me. Real communication like this is how we're going to solve our problems personally, socially, in our neighborhoods, and in our whole communities. We have to actually listen to each other and be in this *together*. We're going to have to talk about how we are the same, not how we are so different.

Each one of us is a unique individual. Still, together, we all share common experiences. We share struggle. We share suffering. Many of us share the desire to benefit the greater good. If you focus only on the "I" as you move through life, you'll miss out on so much connection. When you shift to "we" and start trying to make someone else's life better, it's insane how much better yours will get too.

INSPIRED BY VULNERABILITY

Barack Obama provides a great example of screaming your weaknesses to the world and embracing vulnerability. In 2008, when he was already the Democratic nominee for president, the news broke: Obama's pastor from his youth, Reverend Jeremiah Wright, had made inflammatory racial remarks about white people. Most politicians would have tried to distance themselves from someone like Rev. Wright. They'd try to rewrite history, claim he wasn't important, or argue he was no longer a part of their life.

Obama didn't do that.

Instead, he was open about the situation, stating that Wright had helped him since he was at a very young age. Obama also admitted the reverend had some flaws and qualities of character he didn't like, and he made it clear that he didn't agree with his former pastor.

The key to Obama's response is in its honesty: he stated he didn't like Wright's comments, but he also didn't deny the fact that Wright had been an important, supportive person in his life. Just because he was running for president didn't mean he was willing to cut off someone who'd been like an elder of his family. Obama accepted Wright as a whole person, with good qualities and bad ones. His response made people look at themselves and consider the meaning of relationships beyond political sound bites.

If we're being honest, almost all of us have someone like that in our lives—an offensive uncle, a grandparent who can make off-color comments, or an asshole friend. What are we supposed to do—hate them? We love them and they love us. Despite their flaws, they've been there for us. We probably didn't realize their worst qualities until we were adults. At that point, are we really supposed to kick them to the curb?

Obama's honesty and transparency represent another moment of people being able to say, "Yeah, me too." Love him or hate him, he stuck to his principles. Obama was a polarizing figure, but people also connected with him. That connection is why people were moved to tears when he was elected: white people cried because of the symbol he was, the things he did, and the way he made us feel— like we might actually work together. People like Oprah, my dad, and others in the black community cried because they identified with his struggle. His election was a huge milestone and step in the "we" direction.

HELPING FRIENDS SCREAM THEIR WEAKNESS

There's a difference between weakness and annoyance. If your spouse comes home late from hanging out with friends and totally ignores the stack of dishes in the sink, that's an annoyance. A weakness is all about you and it's all yours. An annoyance goes away when someone else changes or leaves your life. Your weaknesses, on the other hand, don't go away until *you* deal with them. Weakness is like a cancer. It grows and spreads. It belongs to you and no one else.

When I talk to a friend who is struggling, I ask them to tell me their story, weaknesses included. I also make it clear I'm not a therapist; I'm only offering to listen and empathize so they're not alone. I'm not a substitute for professional help, but I can help them get through rough spots, especially if they're waiting to get in to see a professional.

Many people go on medication for anxiety and depression. I'm on medication and I'm not afraid to say it. Still, it's important to note there's more to fixing your problems than medication. If you have high cholesterol and go on a statin, it doesn't mean that now you can be sedentary and eat bacon all the time. You have to make lifestyle changes too. Similarly, you have to put in the work to stop feeling like shit. The work of getting through a breakdown is a lot harder than not eating bacon.

There's no quick fix to overcoming the devil. Going on antidepressants isn't like taking a painkiller. It doesn't instantly make the pain go away on its own. Medication can quiet your emotional pain, but if all you do is take a pill, that pain will come back. Then you'll have bigger problems. Bottom line? The real work is in the screaming.

To fix yourself, you're going to have to scream your weaknesses to the world. That process might start with one person. For me, it was my wife. For you, it might be your therapist. If you see your friend is in crisis, offer for it to be you.

HOW TO START SCREAMING

The suggestions I've made in this chapter won't just help you as an individual. If everyone focused more on connection, honesty, and sharing their weaknesses, we could move through the world with more care for each other. We could raise our children as a village instead of individual households. We can help each other out without expecting payment or immediate reward. Living by these principles can bring us closer together; how can you start this process?

SHARE YOUR SHAME

My friend Scott Strode is the founder of Phoenix Multisport, a drug and alcohol recovery program. Phoenix Multisport is different from an AA program because it emphasizes a physical activity component. Once you have gone forty-eight hours with no alcohol or drugs, you can engage in physical activity with the other participants—climbing, biking, Jiu-Jitsu, boxing, lifting, and so forth.

Phoenix isn't a stand-alone twelve-step program; participants also must go to AA. Still, Scott has created a community that's open, honest, and proud. They have T-shirts and hats they wear with pride, essentially branding themselves as recovering addicts. It's the opposite of the "anonymous" side of AA.

Scott knows a thing or two about recovery, as he is a recovered addict himself. His program is widely successful, and he was even one of CNN's top ten heroes in 2012. He has discovered a way to turn shame into pride—and help people in the meantime.

ADDRESS YOUR FLAWS

Normally, when we're ashamed, we keep that shame right between our ears. Like Scott's program, we need to put the shame out where everyone can see it. Once you know and own your weakness, no one can use it against you. People might try to use it to cut you down, but they won't be able to because you've addressed your flaws.

Sports teams use this strategy. If they're bad at defense, for example, they don't simply pretend they're great defensively. They practice fucking defense! Then they improve. Why? Because they identified and worked on their weaknesses, individually and collectively.

Michael Jordan is a phenomenal example of personal improvement. He came into the NBA knowing he was the best. He was jumping and flying, dunking from the free-throw line, using his athleticism, and crushing all his opponents—just being a great player overall. Father Time catches up with everybody, though. You don't beat him; he beats you.

As Jordan aged, young players entered the league who were faster and could jump higher and farther than he could. He couldn't get to the basket and dunk on five people anymore. He couldn't beat opponents with athleticism alone.

What did he do? He developed the fadeaway jump shot. Players on the court didn't know what he was going to do. Would he fade away where they couldn't reach him and shoot? Or would he make that move and they would defend the fadeaway, letting him get back to the basket?

As athletes get older, they slow down and tire more quickly. But Jordan took what seems to be a weakness for all athletes on an individual level—age—and pushed back on Father Time. First, though, he had to admit his weakness. He couldn't pretend he was still going to have the same athleticism he'd had when he was twenty-two. Instead, he had to say, "You're right. I can't do *that*. But watch *this*."

PRACTICE, PRACTICE, PRACTICE

If you've never screamed your weaknesses, it's understandable to feel terrified at the prospect. In fact, it sounds like the opposite of what you'd want to do. Our animal survival instinct pushes us to compensate when we get hurt and hide that there's anything wrong. An animal with a broken leg goes and hides until it heals, because staying out in the wild means getting killed by a predator. It makes sense. An injured gazelle is the slowest gazelle, and it's the one the lion will catch. Bottom line? No one wants to be the slowest gazelle. If you are, you have to hide or compensate to survive. That's how nature works.

We think hiding will work for us too—only we're not hiding our bodies. We're hiding our souls. That plan may work for a time, but it won't work forever. As you communicate and interact with more people, your weaknesses are bound to show. Humans who are gazelles and humans who are lions live in the same places, on the same streets. If you're a slow gazelle about something in your life, you'd better recognize what's wrong and fix that shit. Then, when the lion comes to eat you, you can say, "Not today, motherfucker."

We're all part of this lion and gazelle fight. Whenever you are the slowest gazelle, own it. I know it's scary to make such an admission. It's not fun. As you fix your gazelle issues, you know the lion could come at any time. Guess what? The longer you put it off, the worse it will be when he does come. And the lion is coming someday, man. You can't fucking help it. The blue fire is where you forge yourself, and the lion is the devil you'll have to fight.

The first time you share your weakness, it will take everything you have. When I got up on the side of the cage and talked to the students at my school, it took everything I had. I felt like I was screaming, but in reality it was likely only a whisper leaving my lips. I was terrified. When I talked to my therapist about it, I was crying.

The next time I screamed my weakness, though, I'd had practice. It was still hard, but it wasn't unbearable. It's like learning to drive a manual transmission, which my grandfather insisted we had to learn growing up. During the war, he had to drive the Nazis around because they didn't know how to drive a stick. Jews who couldn't drive those vehicles were killed. My grandfather's skill not only kept him alive, but he also got some favor with the Nazis in return. They'd even give him a little food or clothing sometimes. In short, driving a stick saved his life.

When you're first learning to drive a manual and you're stopped at a light, it's almost guaranteed you will stall the car out. Then you panic. Everyone's honking at you. That fifteen or thirty seconds you keep stalling out feels terrible. You think, *Oh shit! Oh shit!*

I can still remember the first time it happened to me. My dad was in the seat next to me, yelling at me to hurry up. Those scary, intense seconds are what screaming your weaknesses to the world feels like.

The second time I stalled with people behind me, I didn't panic quite as much, but I still panicked. The third time, I felt a little less panic. Even once I learned how to drive the manual well, it didn't completely prevent me from stalling the car sometimes. Instead, I learned to think, *Oh, OK. I stalled the car. No big deal. Here I go.*

The same process applies to screaming your weaknesses to the world. And no, I'm not just talking about getting on social media and venting, or constantly whining to anyone who will listen. That is not screaming your weaknesses—that is complaining. Screaming your weaknesses is deeper than that because it requires action *after* you scream. You tell people where you are weak, and then you go work on it immediately. You don't just keep telling people. You say it one time, and then that is your trigger to start DBAB'ing.

That first time you do it, though, is like being in that stalled car. Your dad—who is like your heart, soul, and mind—is screaming at you, *Let's go! Let's go!* You're freaking out and sweating. You don't know exactly what's happening or what to do. You're worried about the people honking behind you—your expectations of how you're supposed to be. Everything feels like it's going crazy. At this point, some people will give up and buy an automatic. Not me. And if you're reading this book, not you. We're on this ride together.

Chapter
FIVE

ALL WE HAVE IS NOW

*"You could leave life right now. Let that
determine what you do and say and think."*
—MARCUS AURELIUS

Early in my career, I got cast in the *Ultimate Fighter* reality
TV show. As glorious as that sounds, it was the worst six
weeks of my life, apart from my breakdown.

Here's the setup: sixteen people enter the same house,
and the producers match you up for fights until the field
is narrowed to the final two contenders. You live and
train with the people you're going to fight, which is rare.
I don't fight with my training partners in my regular life.
No way—we help each other get ready for fights.

For the show, though, you're simultaneously training
with and potentially fighting your housemates. You don't

know how the matchups are going to work out. You're all competing for the chance to enter the UFC. Millions of people are watching. You have to make the most of the opportunity, but there's also a weird conflict. On one hand, you're trying to create bonds with people; on the other hand, they're your opponents. You might start a friendship with someone who gets in the cage with you and tries to rip your fucking head off.

The experience was awful, and I'm not the only one who felt this way—we all did. We had zero communication with the outside world for the duration of the experience. I didn't have kids at the time, but I was married. I couldn't talk to my wife, family, or friends. I had no one. There weren't any books, music, TV shows, or magazines allowed. The no-contact rule was designed to breed the type of drama and pressure cooker environment that makes reality shows so popular—and it worked.

The show creators even brought people into the house who weren't the best fighters; they were knuckleheads thrown into the mix to start shit. Behind the scenes, people were peeing on each other's belongings. Someone masturbated onto someone else's food and put it back in the refrigerator. As people lost fights, they stopped competing but didn't move out of the house, so there were constantly assholes partying around me. My roommate lost his first fight, and every night he'd get so drunk that instead of using the bathroom, he'd pee on the floor. I couldn't kick his ass, though, because then I'd be asked to leave.

We found out early on that Dana White, the president of the UFC, was going to take everyone out to a strip club on the last night and give them each $1,000 to spend. People started betting their special strip club money throughout the season. At one point, a bet came up that someone would eat someone else's shit. One night, we were sitting at the dinner table, and someone went into the bathroom, took a shit on a plate, and brought it back to the table. The Federal Communications Commission wouldn't let the show include that footage, but that explains how I lived for six weeks. My main thought every day was, *Are you fucking kidding me?* I was embarrassed. I was married and pretty successful at that point. I didn't want to go to a strip club or deal with anyone's shit—literally and figuratively. I just wanted to fight, and I couldn't believe I was thrown in with these guys.

Besides the interpersonal drama, there was also the stress associated with the fighting and training itself. We were slated to fight three times within the six-week period, if we made it all the way. Normally, I'd fight three times over the course of an entire year, so the accelerated schedule was difficult. Oh, and forget about showing those guys my weaknesses, because they were my adversaries. It was more than a hectic, stressful situation. It was hell.

Unsurprisingly, I started to crumble. As you might guess, I couldn't sleep. I would often lie in bed panicking. Despite it all, I made it to the semifinals, but they were still two weeks away. Being racked with insomnia and genuinely devastated by the whole situation eventually caught up with me. At two o'clock in the morning on the fourth night of not sleeping, I made a decision. *You know what?* I thought. *Fuck this. I'm out.* I decided I was going to quit, even though I knew it would change the course of my life. I'd be ridiculed and ostracized by the martial arts and Jiu-Jitsu communities, but I was willing to accept it. There was one phone in the house, and it dialed directly to the producers. I decided that in the morning, I was going to pick it up and tell them I was done. That I wanted out.

I never needed to make the call, though, because after I got my what ifs out, I fell asleep. That's all it took. The next thing I knew, it was eight o'clock in the morning. I had slept for six hours—more than I'd slept all week combined. Why? I faced reality and then crashed. Everything that was bothering me went away, because I accepted the potential consequences. I knew my struggle was over.

When I woke up, I realized I was back in the game. I

decided I was going to stay. And you know what? Ultimately, that's how I got into the UFC—but I never would have if I hadn't chosen to accept the present moment.

THE HEART OF STOICISM

Stoicism is what taught me that all we have is right now. This very moment. Ideas of the past or the future are merely thoughts you're having in the present. The problem is that too often, we don't live in accordance with this truth. We push things down. We put things off. We think we're immortal and that we have a hundred tomorrows. And I hate to break it to you, but that's not always true.

For many people, the quote opening this chapter feels morbid, but the sentiment is true. Remembering I'm going to die makes me focus on spending time with my kids, my family, and my friends *now*. All we have is today; every day, I strive to balance my life with health, my wealth of knowledge, and love. When it doesn't balance, I know I need to adjust because today could be my last day.

I don't always find the right balance, but I don't let failure upset me anymore. Instead, I try again. If I failed in the last hour, I'll focus on balancing in the next. That's the goal of Stoicism—and much like Jiu-Jitsu, it has saved me.

COMMITTING TO THE PRESENT MOMENT

Recognizing I have only this moment changed my approach to all aspects of my life, including work, family, and fighting.

WORK IN THE MOMENT

I've always been a numbers guy because numbers don't lie. They are what they are, and there's no way around them. I used to obsessively check our customer relations management (CRM) numbers every day because it would allow me to project revenue. I was always worried about what the future held for the business. If we had one hundred members one day and ninety the next, I'd worry obsessively about what happened to those ten members. Where did they go? I had to find out exactly who those ten people were.

There's no CRM program that does a consistently great job at answering those questions. Usually, I could account for those ten members, but not always. Sometimes I could find seven of them, but not the other three. In those cases, I'd spend time on the phone with the company, trying to figure out what happened to those final three even though their loss represented less than 1 percent of our monthly revenue—barely a drop in the bucket. Still, finding those three members would drive me in-fucking-sane. Every morning, I'd wake up in a state of paranoia and immediately check the numbers. I should have been focusing on going to work and teaching the best classes I could every day and prioritizing what matters: creating positive change for students.

Stoicism has given me balance at work, because I've realized that numbers are important to a point, but having faith in the essential goodness of people is more important. If I focus my energy on teaching the best possible class I can in the moment, people will come. Instead of focusing on the statistics, I now know I need to focus on building both my fighting ability and my relationships with our students and team. At the end of the day, people show up because of the relationship you create with them.

MY FAMILY IN THE MOMENT

Seeing I have limited time on earth has also allowed me to put my work down and be more present with my family. When I'm spending quality time with my kids, I don't even think about work. When I'm at home barbecuing, I don't think about work. If we go on vacation, I take my computer every time as if I might work. Then instead of obsessively checking it every morning, I simply don't touch it. Why? Because it doesn't matter. I know when I get back to work, I'll give it my all. I've learned how to commit to the moment I'm in.

I can't give work my all if I don't give my all to my family when I'm with them, and they deserve it. They matter the most. Remember, be the BPP.

I don't expect my kids to want to spend every free moment with me either. Sometimes, they want to go play with their friends, and that's fine too. Still, knowing that I'm available for them at home, supporting and loving them, brings a calmness to my life.

DEFINING MOMENTS

Often, we anticipate an important or defining moment and want it to go well. Maybe we have a big meeting, a job interview, a project deadline, or a high-stakes presentation. A month or more out, we worry about how we'll do. We build defining moments up so much that when they do arrive, they can only let us down.

Think of a bride on her wedding day: she's likely driven herself and her loved ones crazy. She wants everything to be phenomenal, every detail to be buttoned up. Then the day comes—the decorations, the dress, the venue. It's all there. What's not there, though? The joy. Everyone is completely stressed. After the ceremony, she likely feels obligated to have sex because it's her wedding night. Rather than being able to enjoy something—the wedding, or the night, or any little moment in between—the experiences are dampened by what is "supposed" to happen or "supposed" to be perfect. The truth is, every day and every night before that wedding was important too. We often simply don't pay enough attention to realize it.

We have to practice being present for the little moments of our lives, each and every one of them. Of course, it's important to prepare for the big moments, set aside time to think about them, and be in the right mindset to give 100 percent when they come. You can't spend every moment practicing for the future, though. Prepare, then let it go and be there for your family, your friends, and whatever else sets your soul on fire.

This came up for me at a recent competition for a charity organization called Fight to Win. I was in the event for black belts over age thirty. My competition was the five-time world champion master in the biggest organization there is, the International Brazilian Jiu-Jitsu Federation.

I'd done everything I needed to do in preparation for my match. On top of my own upcoming event, a couple of my students were competing that same night. One student was fighting at 6:00 p.m., and my match wasn't until 10:15 p.m. I had to be there for her, so I showed up and coached her. She smashed her opponent and was done in about a minute.

After her match, I still had four hours until my match. In

the past, I would stare at the clock, getting more and more nervous. Instead, I decided to not even look at the time and instead go do something I loved: eat sushi. And I did. I went to the sushi restaurant, shot the shit with the chef, and got back in time to coach another one of my students who fought directly before me.

Many people focus on themselves that close to their own event, but I decided to warm up early and make time to be there for him. I'm no longer a professional fighter; my job is to coach. I put my match aside because, at that point, it wasn't for fifteen more minutes. I coached my student to the best of my ability.

The moral of this story is that by the time my big moment came, I wasn't nervous because I'd kept myself in the present. I knew my 10:15 p.m. fight would be coming all day. I was prepared. I'd done the work. Why let the future 10:15 p.m. moment stop me from enjoying 8:15 p.m.? Or 9:15 p.m.? I was able to avoid obsessing over my nervousness leading up to the fight by living in each second. The alternative? I could have stared at the clock counting down the minutes; we've all done that, and it's miserable. Not anymore.

PREPARATION AND THE LAW OF DIMINISHING RETURNS

For any kind of preparation—for a fight, a work event, a

wedding—the law of diminishing returns applies. Think about exercising: if you do it too much, there's a point at which it stops helping you. Marathon runners run chunks of a marathon in preparation, but they don't run the whole 26.2 miles until the day of the event. It takes a week to recover from the exertion of the full course, and running that far before the event would make them have to *stop* training, not help them perform optimally.

There is a saying in sports: I'd rather be 50 percent undertrained than 10 percent overtrained. When you are over trained, you're stuck in the mud. You can't get out of first gear. When you're undertrained, your engine will still rev just as high; it just won't stay there as long. I'll take that every day over the former.

You'll crush your muscles if you ask them to max out every day. Similarly, you'll crush your brain if you ask it to max out all day long. That kind of constant work and worry simply isn't possible—you'll fall apart. And it's not just you; *nobody* is that strong. Even the most athletic or most successful people in the world don't use up all their energy obsessing. Sure, they obsess sometimes for short periods on some things that matter, but they don't obsess about too much on a daily basis. They'd end up half-assing whatever they'd be doing, and their performance would suffer.

If you're struggling with obsession or overwhelm, pick

three things that have to get done today and give them 100 percent focus. Don't pick ten things—you can't do it. You might think you can, and you might even get them done, but you'll do them at 60 percent capacity instead of 100. Remember, the numbers don't lie. That percentage won't serve you in the long run.

THE ACT OF STANDING UP

It's hard to learn to be in the moment, so start small. Think about what happens when you stand up from a chair. Do you notice the moment you begin to rise? Probably not. Usually, when you're standing up, you're going to do something. You have some purpose in mind. You're focused on *the next* thing. By the time you get there, though, you've missed so many possible moments of intention. Starting with the first moment, the physical act of standing up can help you refocus. That's why I've trained myself to notice the moment I stand up—the literal second my butt leaves the chair.

Picture this: you're going to get a cup of coffee, but that's in the future. First, there has to be a moment when you stand up to leave. Can you notice that moment? Can you count it? Counting stand-up moments is a ridiculously hard task. The most I've ever counted in a day is ten, which is obviously only a fraction of the number of times I stood up. I've challenged my students to do this too; for the first week, the most anyone has ever counted was two.

Counting every time you stand up is a practice. I set the bar low on purpose because if we try too much at once, we're not going to succeed. And, like I mentioned, even this low bar is incredibly difficult.

At its core, this exercise combats our tendency to want to live in and obsess over the future—an act that, ultimately, is no different from anxiety. In both, we wonder, *What if? What's next?* When we live life in the present, we stop "what if-ing" and "what's next-ing" and start "what *is*-ing."

THE MOST POWERFUL MUSCLE

The brain is the most powerful muscle in the body. Why do you think there are stories of mothers lifting cars off their babies? It's the brain that releases the adrenaline to make that happen. On a normal day, there's no way those mothers could lift a car by themselves. When their children are in danger, though, sometimes they can. Our brains have the ability to go into fight-or-flight mode, allowing us to accomplish huge physical feats.

After such a feat, though, the body feels wrecked. We can only imagine how those mothers' physical energy is sapped after the ten-second lift. The point is that after we put our brains in fight-or-flight mode, there's nothing left over. We're done.

If you tax your brain every day, constantly living in the fight-or-flight mode of worrying about big events, you'll be wrecked. Then, when those key moments truly come, the adrenaline will be too much for you to handle. It's not a question of being physically in shape; hormones physiologically cause your body to fatigue. Nobody can handle constant adrenaline spikes and crashes—not a car-lifting mom, not a professional athlete, and not you. Staying in the present moment keeps us from going into fight-or-flight, and part of staying in the present moment is understanding the difference between desire and ambition.

DESIRE AND AMBITION

Desire and ambition sound almost synonymous, but they're not the same: desire is ambition without discipline. Desire is all about the future, and it can come to an end. Ambition, on the other hand, has no end. When desire takes hold, you can lose your focus in the present moment and stray from your why.

When I was fighting in the UFC, I used to have to lose thirty pounds before my fights. Almost all fighters face this scenario; the last week before your fight becomes all about the weight cut. I usually had about fifteen to twenty pounds to go in the last four days. To get through this process, I could eat very little and drink nothing but water and coffee.

Fighters have gotten smarter about this since I retired, but when I was fighting, we basically starved ourselves. I'd eat 500 to 1,000 calories a day and still have to work out two to three hours a day.

It got even worse twenty-four hours before; you'd stop consuming anything, including liquids. You're already starving and then you become completely thirsty too. People would often ask me if I was ready to have a big, juicy steak after I weighed in. My answer was always the same: "No, I want a big glass of water." I knew I needed something basic to stay alive. *That's* desire. I'd have done anything for the water.

A hard weight cut is an example of pure desire because, in those moments, you're not worried about anything but your body and getting through the weigh-in. If things get bad enough, you'll do whatever you have to do to survive. People who are starving will kill each other over a piece of bread. Desire is human instinct, and its power is why it can cause us to break our why.

Ambition, on the other hand, has discipline attached. My

why is being the BPP, which is also an ambition because I have to wake up every day and go after it. It's not just a desire. A *desire* is to get my kids through high school, and then what? My life falls apart? I need more than just a good desire to keep me going.

Desire is a result, and ambition is a process. We're all in the process of being better. I'm in the process of being the BPP and a great husband. I'm in the process of trying to be successful and to help people. When does it end? It doesn't; I have to do it every day, right now.

That's not to say you have to quash your desires. Within ambition, you have to set goals—little steps that might even feed into some desire. We all have to feed our desires sometimes, but they need to take a back seat to the overarching ambition. Have a little ice cream, but live healthfully overall. Even being the BPP, I can't be with my kids 24-7. I allow myself to have some desires along the way, but the North Star always points back to that ambition. Why is this so important? Achieving a desire doesn't bring happiness but pursuing your ambition does. My process of becoming better at Jiu-Jitsu, for example, won't end until I die.

My friend Rashad Evans recently retired from the UFC, and he achieved his ultimate desire of becoming a world champion. The day after winning, though, he felt a huge letdown. He had a shiny gold belt that only a few people in the world would ever have, but nothing in his life was different. He wasn't any happier. After becoming the champion, he told me about how he could never again find the spirit that had driven him to win. He called it the "dirty fucking dog" inside him that made him work so hard. He could never find that dog again.

He also realized he'd fucked up many relationships in his life in the pursuit of fulfilling his desire. Now that his career's over, he realized he mixed up his desire and his ambition a little bit, and he's working on fixing that mistake.

THE GREATEST TEACHER

When someone's trying to choke you to sleep in Jiu-Jitsu—when they're trying to take your soul—you can't focus on anything else. Sure, there's an agreement that if you tap them, they'll stop. Still, you can't help but wonder when you're in that situation, *what if I tap him and he doesn't stop?* The experience forces you into full awareness of the present moment.

You can't think about anything besides dealing with the fact that your opponent's arm is around your neck. Fuck thinking about how it got there. Once you get out or tap him, you can assess what happened. Afterward, you can examine your mistakes. In the moment, though, there's no time for anything except survival. You have to address the arm around your neck and your current loss of blood flow and oxygen.

Then your soul gets taken or you get free. If you get free, you immediately have to address what's going on currently so you don't end up in the same situation again. You can't dwell on being happy or proud of yourself for escaping. A truth about life is if you focus on the past, the same problem will come for you again. His arm will come back for your neck. You can only get lucky and survive that situation so many times if you're looking back or ahead.

When I train, I don't try to beat people. I try to take their soul, because when you take their soul, you take them out of the present moment. And as long as you stay in the present moment while you do it, you win.

Chapter
SIX

HOW JIU-JITSU SAVED MY LIFE

"People would see a lot of times fighting as an ugly thing, as a thing that denigrates the human being. In reality, you see fighting on everything...Everything's fighting. Doesn't matter what it is. You wake up in the morning, to get out of bed is a fight. So, fighting is the best thing a man can have in his soul."

—RENZO GRACIE

The most important lessons in my life have come from getting my ass kicked—from being socially ostracized, to my hardest fights, to my struggle with anxiety. The obstacle is the way, and my struggles have been my teachers.

Life is a fight. Every day, you better wake up and be ready. If you're a gazelle, you have to be ready to outrun the lion each day. You have to learn how to handle life's arm around your neck, choking you out. You have to know how to live in the moment so anxiety and depression don't consume you. The devil finds all of us in time, and if you prepare, you'll know how to handle him when he arrives. The way I learned how to handle the devil was Jiu-Jitsu.

There was a very specific moment when I decided I needed to learn Brazilian Jiu-Jitsu, and it involves my friend John Hasset, who is about fifteen years older than I am. We both excelled in karate, something I'd practiced throughout my entire youth. I went to the national tournament for my style of karate when I was seventeen, and when I entered the sparring division, I noticed that John had entered the old-man division. He was thirty-two at the time. I started to give him shit because when you spar in karate, there's only light contact. It's not like in the UFC, where you try to hurt the other person. In karate, we sparred against our friends all the time. It didn't matter, because we weren't going for knockouts; we were going for points.

"You think I'm scared?" John responded. "Come to my house next Friday night."

"Yeah," I said, "I'll be there."

As a teenaged punk, I had figured I was going to beat this

old man's ass. When I went to his garage, I saw he had mats on the floor. I also saw something else: he was fighting a mutual friend, Jimmy, using a style I'd never seen anyone fight. It was the first time I saw Jiu-Jitsu.

After John and Jimmy finished, it was my turn. John and I fought for about an hour, and as it turned out, he mopped the floor with me. He'd been training for about a year and was still only a white belt in Jiu-Jitsu. We started on our feet, but he put me down and choked me every time. I'd always considered myself a good fighter. Hell, I was a third-degree black belt in karate, and so was he! He didn't use any of those skills in our fight, though. He used his white belt Jiu-Jitsu skills and made me tap out at least twenty times—all this even though I also had thirty-five pounds on him.

After that, it was done. I knew I had to learn Brazilian Jiu-Jitsu.

HISTORY OF THE SPORT

Brazilian Jiu-Jitsu (BJJ) is a martial art that originated in Japan. In the early 1900s, Brazil had a large Japanese migrant population, and one of the best judo practitioners was Mitsuyo Maeda. He went to Brazil and met Gastão Gracie. In exchange for putting him up and helping him acclimate to the country, Mitsuyo had to teach Jiu-Jitsu to Gastão's two sons, Carlos and Helio. He mostly taught Carlos, because Helio had asthma and was frail. Carlos and Helio practiced relentlessly with each other. They modified some of the techniques into what is now BJJ.

Helio gets most of the credit for developing the Brazilian style, though, because he was the one testing the art by fighting all comers. He was only 125 pounds, so he couldn't rely on strength and power. There was no way he was going to get on top of anyone. He had to adapt the moves to fit his condition and use leverage and technique to defeat bigger, stronger opponents.

The brothers developed their skill by fighting all comers. They fought and fought. Opponents would come knock on their door, and they'd stop whatever they were doing to go fight. Eventually, the fighting became wildly popular in Brazil. They'd have events in Maracanã Stadium, a huge soccer arena. They took anyone who wanted to fight, and they didn't have time limits on their matches. Eventually, Carlos and Helios taught the martial art to their sons.

The Gracies, most notably Helio's oldest son, Rorion, brought BJJ to the United States in the late 1980s and was teaching out of his garage. Other people in the martial arts world started learning about this form. In the martial arts community, everyone thinks their style is the best.

There had never been any type of competition to prove this, so it was always ambiguous. In response, the Gracies in America issued something called the Gracie Challenge. They offered to fight anyone from any style, under no rules, and with no time limits. The only agreement was that it would be filmed, and people would be watching. The mystique of this magical art grew and grew.

Rorion got together with some businessmen to create an event so the world could see what the best fighting style was. He called it the Ultimate Fighting Championship, or UFC. The rules were few in number: no eye gouging and no fish hooking. In other words, you couldn't use your fingers to rip out your opponent's eyes or open his mouth. Other than that, it was on.

These events were sixteen-man tournaments. It was simple: whoever was left standing at the end of the fight was the winner. Let's take a minute to understand how difficult this is: first of all, there are no decisions. You have to fight until someone is knocked out or submits. The risk of injuring yourself, even in a win, can be very high, especially since all martial arts up to this point relied on striking.

This is where the beauty of BJJ came in. With BJJ, you take your opponent down, control the position, and then submit them with a strangle or joint manipulation.

Unless they choose not to tap out, both participants can be uninjured.

Rorion's goal was to show that BJJ was the best martial art in history. He got his frail younger brother Royce, who weighed only 170 pounds soaking wet, to compete. There were sumo wrestlers and all kinds of other martial arts champions, and they all succumbed to Royce. When they held the event a second time, everyone fell again to Royce. In the third UFC, he won his match but got beaten up so badly that he wasn't able to continue. In fighting, shit happens.

Royce recovered, and his fourth UFC might have been his most impressive because by then, people had caught on. He went up against a 250-pound wrestler named Dan Severn. Being a wrestler, Severn was comfortable being on the mat, and his style posed a challenge. He was on top of Royce for sixteen minutes, and people thought that would be the end. They thought Royce would fold, but he didn't. Instead, but he caught Severn with a triangle choke hold from the bottom and made the 250-pound monster tap out. From there, the sport took off. Its popularity grew around the world, especially in the United States.

MY TEACHER, THE MAN, AND THE SPORT

After I got beat up by John in his garage, I knew I wanted

to pursue Jiu-Jitsu. I tried to learn about the techniques, but it was difficult because the closest school at the time was in Philadelphia, forty-five minutes away. It was also expensive; I didn't have the money.

Then I moved to Colorado to go to college. I met my teacher, Amal Easton, at a local mall. At the time, he was teaching out of a karate school. I trained with him my freshman year and then I ran out of money. My sophomore year, I heard he opened his own school.

I knew I couldn't afford lessons, but I wanted to see what I could make happen, so one day I asked Amal if he'd trade lessons in exchange for me cleaning the school.

"Man, it's your lucky day," he said. "My cleaner just quit two hours ago." The rest is history.

JIU-JITSU, SUCCESS, AND EGO

I immersed myself in Jiu-Jitsu, dedicating my whole life to it. *Fuck school*, I thought. I still graduated from college and did that correctly, but my real degree was in BJJ.

Over the course of my career, I've been highly successful at the sport. As I excelled, my success helped push the monster of anxiety down and built my ego up. At one time, I was one of the best American fighters ever. That's not true anymore; many fighters came up behind me after I went into the UFC. But at one time, there was nothing I didn't win in the United States. Nothing.

With my bravado and ego, I could be a bully sometimes, especially when I first started fighting. Our gym was a fight gym. We didn't just train to get better—we *fought* every day. We fought each other and we loved each other. We beat the dog shit out of each other. If someone wanted to join the team, they got beat into it. If you kept showing up long enough, then you could be on the squad.

We didn't permanently hurt anybody or knock them out, but new members still took a beating—from everyone, not just one of us. It was part of the bully mentality I once had.

All that bravado built up my ego. At its core, professional fighting is the most selfish thing you can do. It's all about you. It has to be if you want to be successful. When you commit to fighting, it dictates everything you do. The obsession fed on itself and hid my anxiety. I thought I was getting better mentally because I was getting tougher on the mat. My whole image was about just that: toughness. I was getting everything that I wanted in the sport. I was gaining popularity. People knew who I was. Strangers came up to me on the street and wanted my autograph. Reporters wrote articles about me. I was in magazines.

When there was a Jiu-Jitsu tournament, if I was in the bracket, I was the favorite almost every time.

Still, my anxiety problems crept up on me even then. I'd have bouts of insomnia a couple of times a year for a couple of nights at a time. Those nights, I'd pace the floor, waiting to get back to the mat. I've always gone back to the mat.

JIU-JITSU AND INSECURITY

No one's good at Jiu-Jitsu in the beginning. Being bad in this sport isn't like being bad at basketball, cooking, or dancing. In Jiu-Jitsu, when you don't do well, you get beaten up. You don't just score fewer points; another person takes your soul, makes you give up, makes you say, "No more," and makes you declare them the winner. That experience is different from someone playing a little better or dancing a little better than you do. It's not purely physical; it's also emotional. If you suck, you get your ass kicked.

I understand the emotional difficulty of losing at something you've worked your whole life pursuing. When you commit to playing a sport, playing the piano, or trying to be the best at anything, failing is very emotionally devastating. However, within BJJ and fighting, when you lose, there is the added bonus of another man or woman who beat you up. This makes the experience exponentially worse.

On your first day in almost any Jiu-Jitsu school in America, you'll find a 140-pound, fourteen-year-old kid ready to take a grown man's soul. He won't look like LeBron James or seem capable of taking someone down. He might have no strength compared to you and no hair in his armpits yet, but he'll take every ounce of you. Then he'll do it again tomorrow, and the next day, and the next day, until you decide to face your weaknesses. Once you do, every time you come back, you'll get a little better.

First, though, you have to admit what you're bad at. You have to admit that right now, you don't have the skills and need to work on them. Then you put in the work. That kid will still take your soul, but it will start taking him a little longer. You just keep climbing the ladder.

Eventually, you'll take someone else's soul. That activity sounds very dark and dreary, like something that you wouldn't want to try. Still, there's nothing more beautiful than this experience and sharing it with somebody else. It builds camaraderie and trust between two people like no other activity can. Those who take your soul teach you to dance with the devil. It's hell when someone's on top of you. It's even worse when you're giving it everything you have, and you're still simply trying to survive. Jiu-Jitsu puts the devil on top of you and trains you to say, "Yeah, what else you got?"

The only way to get better is to keep coming back and practicing. It doesn't matter if you're having a bad day. You identify your weaknesses and work on them. Either you win or your opponent does. There aren't any excuses. Jiu-Jitsu and numbers don't lie.

NOT LIKE OTHER MARTIAL ART

Jiu-Jitsu helps us break through our barriers because we can practice it at live speed. Other martial arts are difficult to practice live because they rely on punching, kicking, and hitting. Partners training those moves will hurt each other. I can't knock you out every day. But if I stop my punch right in front of your face and say it would have knocked you out, how do we really know? It might have, or it might not.

Wondering how you're actually doing doesn't build real confidence and self-esteem. In Jiu-Jitsu, it's the opposite. When I get my hands around your neck, I don't care what drugs you're on or how strong you are. With no oxygen going to the brain, after five to ten seconds, you'll go to sleep. Everybody will.

We get to practice that every day, yet we don't have to put

each other to sleep. We simply tap out and say no more—a process that works on our humility. You know you can get an arm around your neck and have to tap out. Even as a higher belt, sometimes you'll have to. Sometimes I try something new and make a mistake, and a white or blue belt will beat me. I know I'm going to beat my opponents most of the time, but the mat has taught me that sometimes I won't. That knowledge makes me treat people better.

I use my words a lot better to avoid confrontation. I've learned how to apply the principles of leverage and physical techniques to other parts of my life. I've no longer got the bravado and ego I had in my early years. Jiu-Jitsu has taught me flexibility and resilience through regular practice. It's an intensity that calms everything else down because life's other problems pale in comparison to knowing what it feels like to be choked unconscious. Through fighting, you learn what it feels like to have someone on top of you, trying to kill you. We get to experience dying a little bit every time we tap out. We also learn we can survive many difficult moments through discipline, effort, and staying in the moment.

HAMMER AND NAIL

A key principle that Jiu-Jitsu has taught me is that some days you're the hammer, and some days you're the nail.

We have good and bad days in our lives, and there are also good and bad days on the mat. Everyone starts out as the nail. You get beat on. You get bent. You get twisted a bit. Although your shape changes, the nail never truly breaks. Eventually, if you keep practicing, you get to do some hammering—a much better gig. But you'll only get there if you learn to be the nail first. You also have to remember that someone could always make you the nail again.

The same is true in life. Can you handle getting beat on? Sometimes, as we get older, we think we have life all figured out. We lose our nail skills. Then when we hit a challenge, we don't know what to do. Jiu-Jitsu reminds us that we can never lose our nail skills. Every day, it brings you back to practice. When you bow and step on the mat, all the money you've made doesn't matter. Your great job, beautiful wife, and wonderful kids don't matter. No one cares what kind of car you drive. Your skills on the mat are the only things that matter. Sometimes life crowds in and clouds your mat skills. On those days, you have to learn to be a nail again. Even though you get beaten up, you survive your dance with the devil, and life feels better. On your hammer days, you feel grateful because you never forget you'll be a nail again. The physical risk and the knowledge that you can't be on top all the time are enough to keep you in a heightened state of awareness.

At first, getting your soul taken by a fourteen-year-old

makes you come up with all kinds of excuses. Your ego starts screaming and placing blame on everyone else. People will listen, nod, and shake your hand. Then you'll go again. Jiu-Jitsu doesn't care about all your ego's reasons. As a result, it will save your life—it saved mine.

Jiu-Jitsu is like life: if you don't die young, you get old. You start as a nail, and your nail days will come back around again. My days of getting my ass kicked by twenty-year-old blue belts are coming back for me again. The mat doesn't lie. When I'm fifty and they're twenty, there will come a point when my knowledge can't outweigh their athleticism and youth. My ego had better be able to handle that. It couldn't twenty years ago, but it can today.

JIU-JITSU LESSONS FOR LIFE

Even if you're not in a Jiu-Jitsu match, the hammer and nail analogy still applies. Some nail time is relatively easy to handle. Maybe you're having a bad day with your kids, your spouse is sick, your boss yells at you, or you just feel generally "off." These nail times will pass. Still, you have to realize them, not simply shove them down. Tell yourself, *It's nail time. I'm going to take this beating because I know I can survive it. I've survived worse.*

Other nail times are harder. They last longer and you don't know when they'll go away. Maybe you're anxious, depressed, or addicted to drugs. Maybe you got a divorce. Maybe someone you love passes away, and you're stuck in your grief. Those are the nail days that present more of a struggle. Recognizing the easier nail days instead of denying them helps prevent you from getting bogged down during the harder times.

Ultimately, nails know how to take a beating, which means being OK with periods when things aren't easy or comfortable. Jiu-Jitsu taught me how to go through nail time. When I'm in it and don't know when it's going to end, I am able to accept it for what it is. Nail time is when the universe doles out some humility, letting you know life isn't all cake and ice cream. It's hard. You get scared. Do it anyway.

Jiu-Jitsu taught me to practice being scared, to lean into that emotion. I can feel afraid and compete anyway. I can suffer on the bottom for years and years but keep coming back. The practice has raised my awareness because I know nail time is coming for me again. Father Time is coming for all of us. I won't always be able to beat that fourteen-year-old kid at my school. When he's twenty-four and I'm fifty, he'll be able to tie me in knots. I'm teaching him to be able to make me a nail again. He can't get better without me, his teacher, but he's learning to kick my ass. Those transitions require awareness, humility, and grace.

If you don't handle difficult times with grace, your emotions will run wild. They'll rule your life. With grace, I can be grateful when someone makes me tap out. I can recognize they taught me a lesson when they made me say, "*No mas.*" Even when I don't tap out and they make me suffer, they're teaching me how to survive. They give me a little more fortitude. They can make me struggle, and then we can shake hands, smiling.

INCREMENTAL PROGRESS

Before you win, you have to learn how to avoid losing. The lessons I've shared about Jiu-Jitsu are incremental. Particularly in an age when everyone's social media is blaring how great and perfect they are, it's important to note that improvement, in life or in Jiu-Jitsu, takes time and effort. You don't get your ass mauled on the mat one day and then beat down everyone the next. You don't face the devil of your anxiety or depression one day and wake up fine the next. You have to show up continually.

I'm now a black belt in Jiu-Jitsu, as a result of ongoing practice over time. I'm still using the same moves I did when I started more than twenty-five years ago, but now I'm better at them. There are only two escapes when someone's mounted on top of you: "buck and roll" and "knee to elbow." We teach them to white belts. You learn them within your first three months. I'm still doing only those two moves—there's nothing else. There's no secret. I just had to become excellent at executing them.

When somebody escapes my mount, I know exactly how they're going to do it. They'll do it with the "buck and roll" or the "knee to elbow." If they get out from under me, they're simply better at doing those moves than I am at holding the mount. We know what the rules to the game are, but improvement is a process.

I can't tell you the last time someone beat me with a move that made me ask, "Damn, what the fuck was that?" People beat me with things I learned ten years ago. I know the moves. If I get beaten, my opponent had a better process than I did. That's the beauty of Jiu-Jitsu and why it saved my life: it taught me the process of things. That's why I wrote this book—to help give a little of that back.

And look, I know what you're thinking: *Jiu-Jitsu sounds hard, man.* Guess what? It is. But the vast majority of people who do it don't set out to be champions. Most of my school is made up of those thirty-five and older who don't even realize they're dancing with the devil. They hear about the martial arts we offer and they want to learn. The process is slow, but we take care of people. It's not like we throw people into the deep end of the pool; they find a community that is also willing to do something that's difficult, and they build comradery.

When you practice Jiu-Jitsu, the feeling you get about yourself is amazing. It's an incredible feeling to get yourself out of a mount, for example. You had somebody else trying to keep you down, but you got up. That's a confidence that goes beyond just about any confidence, but getting there takes work.

My school is filled with people who were weak but became very strong because of Jiu-Jitsu. When you start, you go through the process nice and slow; you don't come and dance with the devil right away. He's hidden. When he does come for you, though—when life does hit you—the first thing you start to think about is being mounted and having that guy's arm around your neck. And what do you do? You have to get the hell out of the mount. Jiu-Jitsu teaches you how. It takes a normal, everyday human beings and turns them into superheroes.

CONCLUSION

RIDE OR DIE

"In your darkest hour, when the demons come, call on me brother, and we will fight them together."

—UNKNOWN

My ambition of being the BPP arose from finding my why. I had to have a God, and I found it. To this day, everything I do points back to that single idea. To help make sure I do it to the best of my ability, I've established key rules for me and my boys to follow.

MY COMMANDMENTS

How was I going to raise my sons well? I'm not their God, but I drew inspiration from the idea of the Ten Commandments when trying to create a guide. I decided to develop rules that my kids and I would have to follow:

1. They have to do Jiu-Jitsu.
2. They have to learn to swim.
3. They have to look people in the eye, demand respect, and give it back.
4. They have to be scared and do it anyway.
5. They have to make their money work for them, not work for their money.
6. They have to ride or die with each other.

THE MOST IMPORTANT RULE

The sixth and final rule is the most important: they ride or die with each other. This is the rule that says, simply and powerfully, that if my brother goes down, then I go down. They're connected to each other. As much as they might hate each other and fight at times, they have to be able to depend on each other to be there no matter what.

Part of "ride or die" also means keeping their word and not abandoning people. This rule is essential because so many of our problems, including anxiety and depression, come from not riding or dying with each other anymore. We don't raise our children together. We live in individual houses instead of a community. We see trash in front of our neighbor's house and walk by it, ignoring it, because we say it's not our trash. We're social, tribal beings to our core, and none of us would be here without connections to other people—but as a society, we don't take care of each other anymore.

When humans first evolved, they couldn't be away from their tribe. If you were away from your tribe, you died. Being separated induced panic, anxiety, and depression. We're away from our tribes right now. We're on our computers and phones a lot. We spend so much time watching screens, even when we're with other people, myself included.

Recently, I went to 7-Eleven. As I was at the cashier, I was sending an email or a text. The clerk was talking to me, and I was looking at my phone and talking to her while I typed. Finally, I thought, *Man, what the fuck am I doing?* I was going to be in my car in twenty seconds. At that moment, I was with another individual. I put my phone away and said hello.

We talked for twenty seconds. Her name was Brianna. She's nothing like me. She works at a convenience store and has a lot of piercings. Still, we shared that moment together. I needed to ride or die with her for twenty seconds. The interaction was an easy ride or die, and we need more moments like it. Before I put my phone away, I was blowing it. There's nothing in this world that I've accomplished only by myself—not a single thing. There's no such thing as a self-made man; such a person doesn't exist. Let me say that again: you've done nothing by yourself. You didn't create roads or invent cars so that you can drive to work and make things happen. We like the credit too much today. Somewhere along the way, someone did something for you that enabled you to achieve what you have. Your success results from human connection.

YOUR "RIDE OR DIE" GROUP

We have to help each other and ask for help as well. I go through tough times and I know you do too. I'm not special. I succeeded thanks to my tribe. I leaned on them hard. My grandfather was right: people are either going to turn you in or hide you. I have a couple of people in my life who'd hide me. They'd die with me. You have to have ride or die friends. Not everyone can be that kind of friend—you can't ride-or-die with everybody. But the ones I have mean everything.

Don't get me wrong, sometimes we argue. It's not like I haven't had screaming matches with those in my ride-or-die circle. The important thing is, we get through those days together, we make tough decisions when we need to, and we have each other's backs. No question.

In your life, don't be a sometimes friend, and don't settle

for sometimes friends. There will be hard moments with your ride-or-die group. They might need to tell you you're being a piece of shit, and you might need to do the same for them. It's not comfortable to tell a friend they're fucking up, but that's what real friends do. A ride-or-die friend says, "I love you, and I'm going to go through this piece of shit time in your life with you. You don't have to do it alone."

For example, when I was at the beginning of my most recent suffering, my friend Mike called me. I was not doing well when he called. I was in the middle of hell. We were talking, and he said something very poignant to me.

"Bro, there are a lot of people I'd die for but only two or three I'd kill someone else for," he said. "I'd kill someone for you."

That meant so much to me. I understood what Mike was saying: dying is easy. You die and that's it. Killing someone else is much different. He would have to live the rest of his life with the consequences, both legally and the mental anguish of knowing what he'd done. He was telling me that he was willing to go through all of that for me. That is ride or motherfucking die!

WHAT'S NEXT?

If you've hit this point and realized you don't have people

to ride or die with, remember: DBAB. When I'm connecting with new people, I need to remind myself not to be a bully. I have to back off my bravado, my ego, and a lot of my natural tendencies that can be off-putting. If you're shy, you might need to adjust in the other direction. Don't be a bitch. Whichever camp you're in, the core message is the same: don't let your fear rule you. Be scared and do it anyway.

Second, stop avoiding building community, and stop hiding your weaknesses. It's human nature to want to show off our best qualities. Too often, though, we focus on how we're different. Really, though, I'm no better than you. We're the same. I'm fucked up, just like you. We might be fucked up in different ways, but the underlying condition is the same. And I'm here for you.

WATER YOUR LIFE

If you're struggling, it's easy to think the grass is greener somewhere else. Guess what? It's not. Every place has brown grass. Everybody has some version of their own brown grass beneath the surface. Get your hose out, ask for help, and find a way to water your own goddamn grass. Your situation is not going to change immediately, but eventually, you'll see green again if you do the work and water your life.

As you start to see green sprouts, you'll take pride in what you did. Then you build on that little bit of progress, and you roll with it. The next thing you know, your whole yard might be green. Boom, boom, and boom—it's a snowball effect.

Don't stop there. Don't stop doing great things. I don't know what your great thing is, but share it with everyone. Share your failures with everyone too. When you succeed, try to help another person. Tell them you used to have brown grass. Tell them that you know what it's like to have brown grass. Tell them that you realize you might even have brown grass again someday, and that it's OK. Then walk over to their hose, turn the water on, and start to water their grass!